M000249118

Praise for F
and *The Great Omission*

From American Missionaries/Organizations

I have been a missionary in Western Kenya since 1978. My work is in church planting and the teaching and training of church leadership. In 1993 I became involved with Final Frontiers Foundation.

I believe the local church is responsible to care for their pastor; the Final Frontiers funds are used to go into new areas and start new churches. Hundreds of villages have had the Gospel presented to them with several thousand saved and over 200 churches have been started. I am now working this same program in Eastern Uganda and Southern Sudan. Eleven new churches have been started in Uganda and three in Sudan. The work of the local church is from evangelism to maturity. These funds help pastors return to the new churches to disciple, teach, and train church leaders. Sponsors have helped with bicycles and even motorcycles to help with this church planting program. Final Frontiers' goal is church planting, and I am glad to work with such a program.
— Rev. Randall Stirewalt, Eldoret, Kenya
Independent Baptist Missionary

I can count personal heroes in my life on one hand. My friend, Jon Nelms, is one of them because he has earned the distinction of being a true church-planting pioneer. Long ago Jon discovered that the best way to reach people groups around the world was to invest in national missionaries sent to reach their own with the Gospel of Jesus Christ. What a novel thought! Jon proved the veracity of his convictions by pushing through the naysayers and successfully launching a movement that has helped plant over 36,000 churches. Oh Lord, we need more heroes like Jon Nelms!
— Jack Eggar, President/CEO
Awana®

I've been blessed to know Jon Nelms for more than two decades. One of the things I have always admired about Jon and the ministry of Final Frontiers is their dedication to the cause of worldwide missions and the glory of God. We are honored to partner with Final Frontiers in our outreach to lepers in India.
— Tim J. Ekno, Executive Director
American Education Development.

Jon Nelms has been a friend, advisor, and encourager to us for the past 20 years. In times of need he has challenged and directed us when we seemed to be facing a brick wall. He has sometimes said things that were hard to accept and took time to understand but always were what we needed. He always seemed to understand where we were in ministry and where we should be. Jon encouraged us to print an excessive number of our tract "A Clean Heart for You." As a result, through our tract ministry we have seen hundreds of thousands of people pray to receive Christ as their Saviour and helped supply the needs of many missionaries and national pastors around the world. While sharing with us his philosophy of missions, he has encouraged us to continue to do whatever we can to reach the world for Jesus. *– Larry and Charlotte Franklin, President*
International Children's Missionary Enterprises
Lee's Summit, Missouri

From National Preachers:

Final Frontiers developed in us the passionate desire for planting churches for the past six years and remained the hidden spring of inspiration from day one. Pioneer Ministries thus far has planted 343 churches with a strong spiritual vitality among untouched, unoccupied, and unheard people groups. The Lord is causing His Word to go forth among 14 different people groups; their age-old prejudice against the Gospel is being demolished slowly and is shaping much of their thinking pattern, shaping their character, cultivating purity among themselves, and setting high spiritual goals for themselves.

The method imparted by Final Frontiers has contributed in accelerating the rate of leading non-Christians to Christ, who are being exposed simultaneously to impact their sphere of influence into their own community. We are able to witness rapid growth like that of reproducing churches, multiplying Christians, baptisms, and active witnessing by the new members. *– Rev. Solomon Bijja Satyam*
Pioneers Ministry, Hubli, Karnataka, India

It has been our privilege to know Jon Nelms. He has worked tirelessly for the Gospel in Asia and Africa, and we are thankful for him and for the Final Frontiers. As a pastor and church planter, trained in evangelical seminary in the US, I heartily share Jon's conviction that the greater role of missions must be played by the nationals that are raised up by Godly leaders to reach their own countries.

The natives best know the nuances of the culture of their land (which a foreigner could not easily learn!!) They usually speak three or four languages which could take years for a foreigner to master. One could support 40 to 60 national pastors for what would be needed to send and keep one foreign missionary on the field.

Many in the US are concerned about how to hold the nationals accountable. My answer is, the same way you have to hold foreign missionaries accountable. Train them on integrity issues and observe them. Ask them for regular financial reports, visit their fields, follow the mission work and church planting progress.Jon Nelms and Final Frontiers have done just this!!! We appreciate their vision and labor of love for reaching souls for Christ in regions beyond.

– Rev. Karl Silva, Pastor
Greater Grace Church of Mumbai, Mumbai, India

I am Daniel Sappor, serving as the national director for Source of Light, Ghana branch. As a national missionary working among my own people in Ghana, raising my personal support was the most difficult part of the work as no one knows me and can talk about the work I am doing with others, so as to get people to support the work. I was in this dilemma till 1993 when Rev. Ray Walker of Source of Light connected me to Rev. Jon Nelms and the Final Frontiers Foundation. Through Final Frontiers I was introduced to churches and individuals in the USA who really want to have firsthand involvement in missions by supporting national missionaries. Through the funding I receive from Final Frontiers, many national pastors are also supported, but many more national pastors serving in deprived, rural areas still need support.

The center message of this book on missions written by Jon Nelms can be summed up in this quotation from D.L. Moody: "It is better to train 10 men to do a work than to do the work of 10 men." I conclude by his saying that it is better to support 10 nationals to do mission work than sending 1 person with the support of 10 people.

May the message of this book touch every individual and every church that is out for missions. God bless you.

– Rev. Daniel Sappor
Source of Light, Ghana, West Africa

The way to go is with Dr. Jon Nelms and Final Frontiers. I have known Dr. Jon Nelms for over 15 years. I have proven him to be credible, genuine and committed to the cause for supporting national preachers. I am one who is supported by Final Frontiers.

– Pastor Denis Celestine
National Pastor, Grenada

I am a national director of Final Frontiers Foundation in Russia since 1995. From 1991 until now I do mission work in Russia, preaching on local radio in Moscow as well as a nationwide station throughout Russia and some of the former satellite nations. I believe that Final Frontiers' efforts to support national preachers are not in vain. Ten young Russian preachers were supported by FFF, and they all established churches. But numbers are not so important. I've seen many reports and numbers in my 20 years of service. I also have seen foreign missionaries with very high standards for living yet having very low results. Jon Nelms works with real people, and I thank God very often that I know him, even though we have never met in person, only by phone.

– Pastor Vasily Lastochkin
National Missionary, Russia

Final Frontiers has helped our Indian national pastors through support, and as a result, many souls are being won in India. The help we have received has even encouraged some of our Indian national pastors who were ready to commit suicide due to their extreme poverty. Through *Touch A Life*, the Final Frontiers' ministry is operating two feeding centers in our area, all staffed by our national pastors and their wives. Final Frontiers is also helping Indian national pastors with bicycles, Bibles, building churches, and sewing machines. We are indebted to Final Frontiers in many ways.

It is our wish and desire that with the helping hand of Final Frontiers, soon at least one fourth of India will be evangelized through their supported preachers. Under the spiritual guidance and dynamic leadership of the founder and president, Rev. Jon Nelms, the flag of Final Frontiers will soon fly across India. Bro. Nelms has helped me to build about 40 churches with permanent structures, and more than 150 churches have been built with palm leaves and bamboo with thatched roofs. Every year Bro. Jon Nelms comes to India to strengthen our ministries and to have an open talk with our pastors individually.

– Pastor K. Swatantra Kumar
National Church Planter
Rajahmundry, Andhra Pradesh, India

In 1986 when I went to preach God's good news to the people at one of the big slums at Klong-Teoy, Bangkok, I saw a big American man standing outside of the center building waiting for me. He spoke to me in Thai with the greeting, "Sawaddee-Krab. I am Jon Nelms from the Final Frontiers Foundation." That day our conversation started, and our partnership has lasted until today because we have the same philosophy, and I wanted to do for the Lord Jesus Christ. We discussed how we could reach the sinners to hear the good news of our Saviour Jesus Christ while the door is open. The answer was to train the nationals to reach out to their own people. Thank the Lord for good results with many churches established in many countries through the Final Frontiers Foundation. To God be the glory for the great things He has done!
– Dr. Kiatisak Siripanadorn
Grace Baptist Church, Bangkok, Thailand

Final Frontiers is a great instrument being used by God to bless and support His servants through all the world in extending His kingdom. It is one of the ways God encourages us saying, "I am with you as you serve Me." Glory be to Our Lord and Saviour for the vision given to this ministry called Final Frontiers!
– Pastor/Church Planter, Carlos Messan
University Baptist Church, Tegucigalpa, Honduras

From Pastors

Jon Nelms is a modern pioneer in National Missions. God laid it on Jon's heart to reach the world with the Gospel through national pastors and evangelists when many leaders in fundamentalism were vigorously opposed to this New Testament concept. This man has touched the world for the cause of Christ. I would encourage every pastor, missionary, and missions-minded Christian to read his new book.
– Dr. J. R. Farrington, Senior Pastor
Harbor Baptist Church in Charlotte, North Carolina
Founder of GO WIN Ministries
(Gospel Outreach Worldwide Involving Nationals)

When it comes to missions strategy, Jon Nelms presents it with passion and clarity. When it comes to missions work and strategy, Jon Nelms gets it.
– Mike Newman, Family Pastor
Ventura Baptist Church, Ventura, California

Dr. Jon Nelms' practical and clear teaching on missions not only has energized our membership and strengthened our present missions program, increasing our annual missions giving by over 300 percent, but also has opened our eyes to the needed emphasis on the national church-planting pastor. Having now taken two trips to the field to visit firsthand the church-planting works sponsored by Final Frontiers, I have never been more encouraged at the possibility of fulfilling the Great Commission.   – Pastor Anthony Lamb
Freedom Baptist Church
San Antonio, Texas

Jon Nelms and Final Frontiers came into my life and the life of our church at just the right time. This ministry has supported missionaries since the church's inception (1980). We still send and support career and short-term missions. However, Jon was used of God to open our eyes to an opportunity to be more intimately involved in rural missions—a place where my small support gift goes a very long way. My family is intimately involved with amazing servants of God whom we have never met face to face. But we serve together with them heart to heart. And the idea of supporting a man who is already enculturated in his native situation is just plain smart.

I know Jon, and I know he has no beef with "traditional" missions models but has discovered and developed a way to get a lot of bang for our missions bucks. I also know Jon as a man of integrity, innovation, compassion, and dedication.   – *Roger D. Willis, Pastor*
Lighthouse Bible Church, Simi Valley, California

In 1984 Tabernacle Baptist Church began to work with national pastors. We saw the great benefit in helping these men, but we soon found that they needed supervision and accountability. In praying about the best way to secure their needs, the Lord led my path across that of Jon Nelms. From that day we joined hands in working around the world in sharing the Gospel of Jesus Christ, we have not had a national pastor to resign from Final Frontiers Foundation nor have to "return home" for death, health, or cultural shock reasons. None of the nationals have spent years on deputation, years in language school, nor have had to raise large amounts of money to ship their "goods" to their field.

I would encourage you greatly as you read this book to look at missions from a Biblical, practical way, not in exclusion of American

missionaries but in assisting the preaching of the Word of God to every creature. — *Pastor Steve A. Ware*
Tabernacle Baptist Church, Orlando, Florida

Jon Nelms has been extremely influential in shaping my philosophy of missions. I first met Jon as a young "missionary" at a missions conference in the early 90s. When he communicated his philosophy of missions, and in particular supporting national pastors, I realized at that moment, God was working beyond the boundaries of the Americanized way of missions. You are now holding in your hands that same missions philosophy I was exposed to many years ago. Caution: it will radically transform the way you think about missions.

— *Mark Glodfelter, Pastor*
Walnut Avenue Baptist Church, Pensacola, Florida

Jonny has a love for the national pastor like few others. I have never known anyone who has a better rapport with the national leaders. He respects the "national," seeing him as an equal in God's Kingdom work. He is not their "boss." He is their servant. He washes their feet. He loves them, and they love him! I have learned much from watching Jonny minister to national ministers around the world. I highly recommend you set out to learn from him too!

— *David Nelms, Pastor*
Grace Church, West Palm Beach, Florida

Final Frontiers Foundation's efforts to find supporters of national pastors allows our church to build and strengthen the church in areas where the Gospel has not already gone, where national Christians are already busy with the work of the harvest.

Our church was introduced to Final Frontiers Foundation in 2004, and we have been supporting national pastors since then. We appreciate the degree of accountability, transparency, and efficiency at which this ministry operates. We have taken three "visionary trips" with Jon Nelms to Honduras to visit and encourage one of the national pastors we support. We have discovered that Jon's heart beats for the spread of the Gospel through established and doctrinally sound national pastors. — *Pastor Darren Lemmon*
Medina Federated Church, Hudson, Michigan

From My Pastor

I truly do thank the Lord for the wisdom that he has given my dear Brother Jon Nelms, especially in the area of missions and world evangelization. I have struggled for years with the amount of money that our church was "wasting" by supporting men who either did not make it to the field or stayed for a very brief time. Some of it may have been due to health issues, family needs, but for the most part, it was due to the culture shock that took place. I have been praying for a very long time about the best way to still support men whom the Lord has called from America to go to foreign soil, as well as supporting men from other countries who know the culture, language and have a heart for their people. Brother Nelms' ministry with Final Frontiers was the answer to my questions. Now we have a very balanced and supportive system in place, and we are seeing the benefits of supporting missionaries from both sides of the spectrum. I am so thankful for the ministry of Final Frontiers; it has helped me understand more clearly the Great Commission.

Brother Nelms and his staff are members of the church that I pastor here in Augusta, Georgia. Our church and the ministries here are enriched because of the service to the Lord. I count it an honor and a privilege to be the pastor of these dear brothers and sisters in Christ. In addition to being pastor, I have also traveled to several foreign countries with Brother Nelms and have seen the work firsthand. I am happy to report to you that the work of the Lord is being carried out in many nations by national pastors. I have met many of our brothers in the Lord's work and have great confidence that they are truly faithful soldiers of the Lord.

The work that Final Frontiers does in raising support for these men, our brethren, is greatly appreciated by them and their families. I have seen how they receive and respect Brother Nelms, and my heart has been blessed many times over to see how they long to have a church sponsor them.

Brother Nelms and Final Frontiers has helped me "get it" when it comes to supporting national pastors while still helping men from our USA who are called of God to go to the regions beyond. Jon's heart is both deep and wide when it comes to helping churches and national pastors fulfill the Great Commission.

– Donald C. Prosser, Pastor
Providence Baptist Church, Augusta, Georgia

The GREAT OMISSION

Why we have **failed in accomplishing** our
Master's departing command of **global missions**,
———————————{ AND }———————————
How we can be the **first generation** in history
to **finally** and **fully** accomplish it

JON NELMS, *Founder of Final Frontiers Foundation*

ISBN: 978-09-831153-1-1

First Printing–March 2011

Scriptures are taken from the King James Bible.

To order additional books, contact:
PHALANX MEDIA NETWORKS, LLC
1200 Peachtree Street
Louisville, Georgia 30434
www.phalanxnetworks.com
publishing@phalanxnetworks.com

or at www.TheGreatOmission.com

Printed and Bound in the United States

Dedication

I humbly dedicate this work...

- to the unnamed and unknown missionaries whose sacrifice, efforts, patience, and persistence have planted the seeds of the Gospel across the world and yielded a bountiful harvest. Without you, there would be no national church planters.

- to the national church planters whose instruction has taught me, whose testimonies have inspired me, and whose lives have motivated me to give my all for our Lord's Great Commission. You are truly those of whom the world is not worthy, and it is my great honor to be your servant and friend. Without you, there would be no need for Final Frontiers.

- to my family, staff, and ministry partners who have struggled and survived victoriously with me. You have been my encouragers, my tutors, and my motivators to carry on when circumstance and condemnation urged me to quit. You have truly done the laborious work of the ministry while I have simply done the ministry. Without you, there would be no Final Frontiers.

Persecution

- *Did you know* that more than 70 percent of all Christians now live in countries that are experiencing persecution?

- *Did you know* that over the last 20 centuries, and in all 238 countries, more than 70 million Christians have been martyred—killed, executed, or murdered—for Christ?

- *Did you know* that more Christians have been martyred in the last 100 years than all years since AD30 combined?

Acknowledgments

I have always read the acknowledgments, seemingly from a sense of duty, in order to recognize those who contributed what I felt was the mundane and insignificant work of editing, proofreading, and project completion. It was, I thought, merely the author's way of expressing a mandatory "thank you" to his small team of helpers whose expertises make him look good.

Now that I have entered the world of authorship, I have come to understand that without these people, there would be no books. In my mind, or what there is left of it, is a myriad of facts, suppositions, opinions, statistics and philosophies, buried so deep in the wrinkles of my brain that they will never see the light of day (hopefully). I know they are in there; somewhere, I just can't seem to let them out in a sequential order that will allow others to benefit from them.

As I sit hour after hour making valiant attempts at clarity, I find myself circling the wagons as the Indians of confusion and repetition shoot their arrows at me with ever-increasing accuracy. When all seems lost and the dark clouds of inadequacies are raining on my gun powder, I am revived to look up and see the cavalry of editors and proofreaders galloping to my rescue. Among them are...

Linda Stubblefield, along with her husband David, have somehow brought reason to my ramblings. They have truly made me believe that mind reading exists. I offered Linda a manuscript that she has turned into a book. Like a lifeguard, she jumped into the sea of my confusion at her own peril. She surfaced from time to time gasping for air as the unceasing undercurrents of my thoughts sucked her deeper and deeper into the abyss; but like the savior she truly is, she fought her way to the shore, and with her came the exhausted body of work, safe and secure, that had nearly drowned her as well as itself. Thank you, Linda. Now take a vacation; you deserve it.

Then on her trusty steed named Grammar, Rena Fish jousted with every dangling participle and split infinitive scattered throughout the pages. Her greatest triumph was won over that evil black knight of repetition from the Land of Infinite Commas. How could she slay such a beast who seemed to multiply itself each time she struck it down? What a great mystery, one worthy of a book of its own to be sure.

I must also express my utter surprise and gratitude to Heather Black, who somehow reached inside my mind and pulled out a cover image that expresses the thought, planning, and preparation that goes into finding and reaching those final frontiers of the earth still waiting to hear, for the first time, the name of Christ. Heather, I hope that was just a fluke because if not, your husband will never be able to hide a thing from you! You are truly a talent artist. I am so glad you use your gifts in our Master's service.

Then there are the numbers who have bugged me for years to write. I hope you're satisfied now! This may not be what you were looking for, but before I can entertain you with stories of great national preachers and their sufferings and triumphs, I must first lay the foundation for why we support them in the first place. Don't be despaired, work has already begun on that project. I have written at your request, and I have done so not because I finally have something to say but because I feel I have finally earned the right to say it.

In 1994 my brother David encouraged me to write a book about my philosophy of missions. I told him that I hoped to someday do so, but not until I had at least ten years' experience. Many at that time were calling my philosophy a "nice theory" but suggested that in time, I would come to my senses and reform my erroneous opinions. So I waited. The years passed by—15, 20 and now, after 24 years, I finally feel that I can say something that the church needs to hear. I hope I am right as I write, if for no other reason than to honor those of you who have encouraged me and waited so patiently. Now get out there and buy a bunch of these books so I can do it again!

I also wish to acknowledge those who have taught me, mentored me, and shaped my philosophies and life. I want to give honor to the thousands of national preachers and church planters, as well as their missionary counterparts who have been my examples and inspiration in my "reasonable service" to my Lord and Master.

I want to say thank you to my departed wife Juanita, who was with me from the beginning of this ministry to the beginning of her eternity. I miss you and so deeply appreciate the strength that you loaned me to carry on when everyone told me to sit down and shut up. You endured the "days of small beginnings" quietly and faithfully in the shadows and now have your reward in a place where I cannot get my hands on it to spend it. Thank you, Babe. See you soon!

I want also to thank my children, Daniel and Sara, who grew up almost without a father. You have shared with me in the toils and suffering from day one and know how real that suffering was. You have endured years without me and months with fevers and typhoid, malaria and a host of other illnesses, both mine and yours that you suffered for the Name. I honor you and know that without you and your spouses, Nolvia and Michael, there would be no book to be written, only a tale of failure.

And finally I gratefully acknowledge the contributions of my new wife Nolin. How precious you have become to me and how comforting you are. Your blind support has been a strength to me on this journey. I only hope that you never learn how wrong you are about me and that I will someday be the man, the minister, the missionary you believe me to be.

Now for those of you whom I have forgotten, you know who you are, and I apologize for skipping over you. Send me a check, and next time I'll remember you. Finally, I wish to acknowledge the sponsors of our ministry: those families and churches that give faithfully to support their chosen preacher, child or project, certainly, without you we would not exist. I remind myself continually that it is the preachers who do the work for which we receive the acclaim, and it is you who pay for it to be done. I just stand in the middle and get the credit and applause from both sides, deserving it from neither. What a great life I have!

Table of Contents

*Despite God's command to evangel-
ize, 67 percent of all humans from
A.D. 30 to the present day have never
even heard of His name.*

UNIT 3: Fixing the Problem

Foreword

by Dr. Ray Young

Did you know that United States Christians possess or control trillions of dollars while on any given day over 200 million Christians in the third world are starving?

D r. Jonny Nelms is not a man who is trying to use a book to propose a theory that he feels confident will work if someone would try it; he is testifying of what he has personally seen God do during his lifetime as a full-time servant of God. In the introduction to this book, Brother Nelms uses the words "my world—the world of missions." These words, in my opinion, truly tell the story of his life. If one knew all that God has done through this great man, he would understand and endorse the legitimacy and reality of these words "my world—the world of missions." Since 1986, Final Frontiers has raised and provided financial, administrative, on-sight logistics and involvement support for over 1,400 national pastors and/or missionaries in 84 different countries. The combined efforts of these who are supported, sponsored, trained, and held accountable by the Final Frontiers Ministries have to date (February 2011) started over 36,000 churches somewhere in the world. As this manuscript goes to press, these numbers continue to multiply at an ever-increasing rate. This book is not just another book that simply states the obvious. This book is a well-written treatise that, I believe, will be used of God to provoke laymen, pastors, missionaries, and Christian financial donors to rethink, reorganize, and reaccelerate their resources, energies and efforts for the cause of Christ. All of these truths are revealed in this well-prepared, Spirit-filled document.

I first met Dr. Nelms as a fellow student at Hyles-Anderson College. Upon our graduation, I lost track of Brother Jonny until recently. Dr. Nelms did not seek me out for help, sympathy, or even glory. I sought him out for the sake of an old and somewhat uncultivated friendship. Basically, I had heard of Dr. Nelms' outstanding work and wanted to hear firsthand about his labors in the field of missions. My, was I ever pleasantly shocked to see what phenomenal things God has done through this giant of the faith. Here are some of the facts that I discovered in my search.

He has had over 25 years of experience in the field of missions without fanfare. He has traveled extensively. These trips were not just short, pleasurable trips to visit well-established missionaries who had already succeeded, nor were they just a few nights in a five-star hotel with short excursions of a mere few hours per day. No, I am speaking of a man who has spent weeks, months, and even years in primitive conditions helping to establish churches all over the world.

Dr. Nelms has been threatened by knife-wielding natives who had never before seen a white man. He has been attacked by giant, swarming ants. He has been nearly engulfed by clouds of malaria-infested mosquitoes. He was brought to the brink of death one night by sustaining multiple scorpion stings. He has been adversely affected by food poisoning, broken bones, malaria, typhoid, pneumonia, and other tropical and devastating diseases while establishing these mission churches all over the world.

He has led scores of groups into and out of different mission fields. He has built with his own hands many mission buildings. He has negotiated the release, arranged the method of passage, and orchestrated the clandestine escapes of captured, would-be martyrs from multiple countries. He has organized and implemented the smuggling of hundreds, yea, thousands, of Bibles into countries and regions which are labeled as "closed" to the Gospel, religion, and the Word of God.

He has trekked through jungles, slashed through tropical rainforests, climbed mountain trails, crossed sun-scorched wastelands, and navigated the narrow passages of crowded, third-world metropolises just to plant a New Testament Baptist church.

He is a very intriguing speaker. He is sincere, well-spoken, and at times humorous. As a writer, he is also intriguing and interesting and even more effective because the reader can pause, ponder, review and digest each thought-provoking and truth-revealing phrase, statement, or paragraph.

It has been my sincere pleasure to have the opportunity to introduce to you this humble, dedicated servant of God and his life-changing manuscript.

– Dr. Ray Young, President
Hyles-Anderson College

• *Did you know* that Christians spend more on the annual audits of churches and agencies ($810 million) than on all their workers in the non-Christian world?

• *Did you know* that the percentage of Christian resources in countries that are already more than 60 percent Christian is 91 percent? Did you know the percentage spent in countries where less than half the people have EVER heard of Jesus is 0.03 percent?

• *Did you know* that Christians worldwide spend an estimated $8 BILLION dollars PER YEAR going to the more than 500 conferences to TALK about missions. That's more than HALF the total spent DOING missions.

Preface

Did you know that the current world-wide ratio for the support of national missionaries compared to the foreign missionary is 100 to 1?

M any ministries today make a point of stating that they "work with the nationals." I can remember when such a statement was a mark of derision. Today, however, if a missionary does not include that in his policy, no church will assist him; after all, that is what we as missionaries are supposed to be doing. Unfortunately, most of those who make such a claim have not altered their ministries in the least. It is just now necessary and popular for a missionary to state he "works with the nationals." Such work could mean only that he provides curriculum or builds buildings. These are worthwhile ministries, but often the only change in the program is that now, in order to be considered a "real missionary" and be funded, the missionaries have to swallow the fact that their boards oppose supporting nationals and imply that they are there to help the nationals rather than to build their own ministries.

Others work hand in hand with the national preachers while maintaining a superiority over them and, in many cases, a non-biblical control of these men and their ministries. Still other boards have now adjusted their positions by allowing the national missionary to get support if and only if he will come to America and raise it for himself as American missionaries do.

Somehow these boards feel that stance is acceptable, but a ministry that raises support for nationals so they don't have to come to America (like Final Frontiers) is unbiblical.

Final Frontiers feels we are better at publicizing the works of nationals than they are as far as raising support goes—especially those who don't even speak English. They are certainly better at reaching their own people than we are—especially those of us who do not speak their language. Besides, every month a national preacher is in America raising support is a month he is away from his family and ministry and a month that he is not doing what God has called him to do. And while most nationals could raise sufficient support from one or two churches, there is that tendency to remain to raise more and more. In the end, he returns home a stranger to his own ministry and alienated from his peers because he now has support many times greater than the rest of them put together. Of course one may wonder, does he not share his surplus with the other preachers? In fairness, one must consider: was he ever given such an example to follow by his foreign counterparts?

Final Frontiers is different and has been from day one. We don't work with the nationals; we work for them. We are not their boss; they are ours. We are not there to teach them; we are there to be taught by them and to help them effectively extend their teachings to their own people in whatever way they direct us. Agencies have made many mistakes over the years regarding such partnership in missions, but that is no reason to "throw out the baby with the bathwater." In most cases, these mistakes were made because the agency was not thorough with their investigation of the national preacher before they began support, nor have they been consistent with accountability since.

Fundamental missions agencies have for decades fought Final Frontiers and similar organizations on this concept of supporting national missionaries. They have mocked the concept and written articles on "Why It Is Unbiblical to Support

National Preachers" without ever giving a single verse of Scripture to support their claim. Now these same men teach missions classes in our Bible colleges and gain millions of dollars from our churches to support their own missionaries. Still, they insult the national preachers and leaders as uneducated, backward, Biblically ignorant and undeserving of funding, claiming that they will be ruined by support and that it weakens the national church. Yet in spite of this, they now claim that they "work with the nationals" when in reality, nothing has changed. In the meantime, we at Final Frontiers have faithfully performed the call God put in our hearts in September 1986, and our "theory" as it was called by some mission board presidents has now become common practice. Even today, American missionaries on deputation no longer just refer to themselves as "missionaries" but rather as "church-planting missionaries." Church planting is a philosophy that I have long taught and is what qualifies a man as a missionary in the first place.

Now there are hundreds of similar ministries that "work with" and even a few who "work for" the national churches. I believe that through research, wise counsel, and more than 24 years of experience, the Lord has given us an insight into overcoming these hurdles which has been proven successful and copied by multiple other agencies. We are thankful for all who have found the truth of Biblical missions but rejoice that God led us into this field as pioneers—when no other man had laid a foundation for us to build upon.

We pray that our methods and ministry will continue to inspire others to walk this trail with us, and it is our hope that this book will clearly explain who we are, what we do, why we do it, and how effective it is.

Final Frontiers was founded in 1986 as the first Baptist missions organization created for the purpose of supporting national church planters. As of 2004 Final Frontiers has been listed by the Evangelism and Missions Information Service as the second largest Baptist missions organization in America and the fourteenth largest of all missions organizations, dwarfing entire denominational agencies like the United Methodist, Presbyterian (PCA), Church of God, etc.

At our current rate of growth, we could become the largest sometime in the next 20 years. Already we are the largest missions organization in a number of countries and still the only Baptist organization in others. Our combined attendance in the churches we have started is more than 4.5 million weekly. Currently Final Frontiers supports church planters in some 84 nations. The day of fundamental missions taking a back seat to all others is finally over.

❖

The following is an article reprinted from the first quarter 2011 Progress Report. Previous articles can be seen in the archives of our Web site at FinalFrontiers.org.

The Ever Expanding World of Final Frontiers

Each year in January we give our partners and supporters a look at what was accomplished in the past 12 months and over the life of our 24-year-old ministry—kind of a "State of the Ministry" report.

As our ministry grows older, we are often tested and tempted with new opportunities of service. It is easy to get sidetracked in life and ministry, forsaking what is best for what is good. Part of my responsibility as the founder of this ministry is to ensure that all we do leads to our primary purpose of church planting. Examples of such ministries are our *Touch a Life* and *Daily Bread* ministries to hungry children. They enhance the work of the local churches and can provide income to the pastor's wife as a supervisor, as well as feeding the children of the pastors. Sometimes it is difficult to get a pastor sponsored, but we can usually get all of his children sponsored easily. This accomplishes the same thing for the most part (support for the church planter) and keeps us on our course.

Naturally, the most important "thing" that leads to the starting of new churches is the direct support of the national church planters. From day one, in fact even before day one, our mission statement has been: ***"Through the funding of national preachers, we endeavor to effectively advance the gospel where it has never been preached before."*** It is simple and so direct that several other organizations have practically plagiarized us, using it as their mission statement.

I have been delighted over the years to see many other ministries spring up, driven by the same motivation. There are times when I have felt it would be better if some of them had just worked with us, an already established ministry, rather than launching out into the deep on their own, especially if the motivation was something as shallow as ego or wanting to use a particular name they evidently feel dropped out of Heaven and must be used. Still, I am nevertheless ecstatic for those who did launch out into the deep, cast their nets, and have drawn in a great catch. We have always done what we could to help such new ministries by teaching them our methods and giving them the same training we do for our own new representatives. That is because we are in competition with no one but ourselves, and if I can shorten a brother's learning curve and help him to benefit from my mistakes, grow faster, and be more effective, then I am pleased to do so.

Even today there are men who contact me wanting to start their own ministry who desire to benefit from our years of experience. I am always happy to help, but I suggest they consider partnering with us rather than going on their own as the expense and time maintaining accountability is overwhelming

There are many American pastors who after taking a missions trip wish to start their own ministry. To them I would say, "count the cost" or you will be like the man who started to build the tower and was not able to finish. Pastors have good hearts and want to help their struggling, destitute counterparts overseas. But they often don't realize the enormous load of accountability that comes with this type of ministry and are unable to bear the burden. They find themselves being double-minded and unstable in their ministries because they are trying to be a shepherd and, at the same time, trying to be a missionary. The two do not necessarily mix over a long term. In the end their vision of an expansive ministry shrinks to five or ten overseas preachers who are supported by their single church. They go back and visit each year but can never expand in territory or in numbers because their pastoral duties limit their ability to administer and their opportunity to go out and raise support for others. To do these things would require that they be away from their church for extended and frequent periods.

A pastor cannot shepherd the sheep from afar. He starts a good ministry, but he could accomplish so much more working with us or a ministry like ours that is in the business of doing what we do and is not pulled aside by the ministry of pastoring. Then all the hours he gives to "missions" could be spent in training and equipping the men he loves so much, while others take the responsibilities of accountability and fund-raising. That is what we do, and by God's grace we do it quite well.

Planting churches is the work of missionaries, and supporting those men, enabling them to do a better job at what they are already doing, is the work of Final Frontiers. Those who spend their time doing other works unrelated to church planting are quite frankly misusing the term "missionary." The Apostle Paul, through his teaching and his actions, taught us that the work of a missionary is to take the Gospel to the ethnic groups that have to this point been unexposed to the Gospel. His primary ministry focused in what we would today call Turkey, Syria, Rome, and Greece, though some believe it extended throughout all of Southern Europe, all the way to Spain and north to England.

We know that Paul preached in a dozen or so cities in these regions and then declared that his task had been completed and that he had nowhere else in that region to preach. It was for that stated reason he planned to go on to Spain. Yet we know that in that same region there were hundreds and perhaps thousands of cities, towns, and villages that had not yet heard the Gospel. So how could he declare that he had finished his job? Simple really. Paul was a missionary, and missionaries are tasked by Heaven as being the ones who go first to an ethnic group to expose them to the Gospel and to plant a church among them. That is why Paul declared that he did not build upon another man's foundation. Paul, as a missionary, did not go where others had gone; rather, he went where others would follow. In Ephesians chapter four, he gives us God's order of expanding and maturing the church, declaring that behind the *apostle* (the Greek word for "missionary") comes the evangelist. His job is not primarily to plant the seeds of the Gospel, though he does so on a regular basis as we all should, but he is gifted and tasked primarily with reaping the harvest. There may be a small church there when he arrives, and by small, I mean a house church or gathering of a dozen or so new believers who were baptized by Paul the missionary.

Before he had left this tiny, new infant church, he appointed elders to guide and protect them. These were not scholars; they were themselves new converts who had shown a rapid maturity in the faith, and he set them up to be examples for the others to follow. But he would also leave some of his team there to help grow the body as he moved on to plant his next church. When later they were joined by *prophets* (traveling preachers) and a pastor had been appointed, they, like Timothy, could move on, catch up with Paul, and begin anew their same function in a new location.

Others, like Titus, would "stay in Crete," having such a deep love for the young church that he could not tear himself away from it. His missionary days were over as he assumed the task and title of a "pastor."

It was not necessary for Paul to preach in every village in order, from his perspective, to declare a region "reached." What was necessary was for him to find a cultural center or ethnic center, if you will, from which a planted church could serve as a launching pad to reach every village and town in that ethnic group and thereby eventually present the Gospel to every person within that ethnic group. Paul was not there to finish the job; he was there to finish his job as a missionary—which was to penetrate a culture and plant the seed of the Gospel that others could come behind and multiply (evangelists), cultivate (prophets) and mature (pastors).

This is one area where we stray from Biblical principles in our missions work and philosophy. We allow the missionary to stay in one location for life, continue to call himself a missionary, and be supported as such. He is not. He may have been, but he no longer is. He is now a pastor, pastoring in a foreign location. But he is a pastor nonetheless and should be supported by his church primarily, not by missionary support from America.

There are those who say we hurt the national church by supporting their preachers because by doing so they never learn to support them. The concern is that they have no pattern of doing so to follow. If that is true, then we certainly do the same by supporting missionaries whose salaries are perpetually provided by American churches, decade after decade, though they pastor a singular church.

Can you imagine what would happen if the churches in the United States actually did change their philosophy of support, giving missions support only to church planters? First, many missionaries would be encouraged to continue planting churches, realizing that that is their calling, not pastoring. For those who chose to pastor, their support funds could be freed to support more actual church planters. These overseas American pastors (those who are called missionaries for the most part) would then have to become legal residents of their host nation so that they could work and receive a paycheck from their churches. This would solidify their commitment to that land and demonstrate their love and determination to live and die with those people. We expect aliens living in America to show that commitment by establishing their lives here as legal residents, not perpetual tourists. Why should we not do the same when we move to share the Gospel in a land that we claim God has called us to? If so, missionaries, once they arrive on their field, could do as Cortes did on the shores of the Yucatan. Gather your men on the beach and burn the boats in their sight so they (or you) see that there is no going back, no hope of retreat or escape—only advancing forward to victory or death as you storm the gates of Hell.

This is the pattern we have followed in our church planting efforts, and it has worked. Let me illustrate: the statistics, all verified and supported by documentation, illustrate the advantage of working with and supporting national church planters. They do not by any means suggest that an American missionary should not be supported, even though the funds it takes to support one of "us" will generally support one hundred of "them"; it is certainly no sin to support any servant of God who is doing the work of a missionary. The "sin," if you want to call it that, is of being a poor, unwise steward and supporting a man as a "missionary" who is only a preacher or pastor. Support him as such if you like, but don't call him a missionary.

Calling a man a missionary just because he has moved from pastoring in America to pastoring in Armenia does not make him a missionary. It diminishes the Biblical definition of the term, it diminishes the qualifications and sacrifice of the office itself, and it bypasses God's order for the maturing of the saints for the work of the ministry. It also consumes the precious few missions dollars designated for missionaries, diverting them to professional, career pastors serving on a foreign field (or dare I mention serving in another state other than the one in which they grew up in America).

Over the years we have striven to assure sponsors that the funds they give for a church planter not only get to the man they have chosen but are used for that purpose, and if he fails to continue in that calling, they are notified so that they can redirect their "missions dollars" to a man who is doing missionary work. Following this policy assures we support only church planters—men who are actively and consistently involved in church planting and training others for the ministry. That is why we have the results that we have. We are not just supporting national preachers but rather preachers who specialize in planting churches. Some may hold the title of a national pastor, but as Paul told Pastor Timothy to do the work of an evangelist, these national pastors also do the work of a missionary. It is for those labors that they qualify and receive support from us. So when you think to yourself that we have an enormously high number of churches planted each year, you can understand why. We support church planters—nothing more, nothing less, nothing else.

Some wonder still how these men can be so effective in their ministry. It is because they are trained to use a Biblical format and to adapt their methods to their own cultures. We do the same here Stateside. In America if someone wants to start a church, he simply rents an office space, prints a flier, passes it out around town, and waits for people to come in on the grand-opening Sunday. Generally, those who come are disgruntled former members of another local church. That is the American way of planting a church. Here in America, we don't multiply; we divide.

In third-world nations, planting a church has nothing to do with a facility, a flier, or a schedule. It involves door-to-door soul winning, street preaching, and one-on-one witnessing until a nucleus of newly saved and baptized believers has been developed. Then the church planter begins meeting with them regularly each week and even more often to teach them God's Word, train them how to witness to their families and friends, and begin to mature the body. If the man is a pastor, he stays; if he is a missionary, he finds a pastor to come and take the little flock and mature it. The church planter selects two or three

Introduction

Did you know that an estimated 70,000 people are converting to Christ each day throughout the world?

Recently I had a prolonged conversation with a group of pastors—one of many such meetings I have had across America over the past couple of decades. After listening to the various pastors vet their discouragements and disappointments with their church's missions program and missionaries, one of the pastors summarized the condition better than any I have ever heard. "The truth is," he said, "the whole missions program of our churches is broken, and no one has the courage to tell it like it is and provide a solution."

The whole purpose of my writing this book is to help churches to be more involved in accomplishing the goal of world evangelism and to give guidance and suggestions on how to fix that which is broken. Missions and missionaries are considered the "sacred cows" of modern churches, though by financial statistics, that devotion is generally more "lip service" than reality. Missions is something many churches do once or twice a year to raise a missions budget and then give it a booster shot when the pledges slack off. It is not the central thrust of most ministries, and most would say that it should not be. Missionaries are generally not brought in to give the church people a burden or to enlist new missionaries. More often than not, they are looked upon as "hired guns" brought in to tell moving stories and raise funds. Perhaps there is some justification for this since that should be among the things that a missionary does best. The last thing that many pastors want a missionary to do is to challenge his church members' thought patterns or to give suggestions on how to do missions better or maybe even Biblically. Neither does the pastor want the missionary to suggest— even by osmosis—that the church may be supporting, among some excellent men, others who are lazy, unproductive, and dishonest. It's perfectly acceptable to reveal such deficiencies about a politician, a television evangelist, or a local pastor whose ministry is growing faster than his, but how dare anyone be critical of a missionary! And if the one doing the criticizing happens to be another missionary, so much the worse for now he has become a traitor.

Baptists have historically been among the front runners of the missionary movement, including William Carey in India, Adoniram Judson in Burma, and others who followed them and have, in many cases, led the way. Thank God others have also picked up the ball and have run with it. But even collectively the fulfillment of the Great Commission has still not been accomplished.

When Baptists and Protestants reignited missionary work several hundred years ago, no one really knew what to do or how to do it. The goal for missions had more to do with proclaiming the Gospel than the methodology of how it might perpetuate itself. I am glad that they were so zealous, and I praise God that such zeal remains and even increases to this day. Still we must now begin to look beyond the burden of the proclamation to the method and means of accomplishing it, so that fulfillment of the Great Commission is no longer dependent upon the blond-haired, blue-eyed, white-skinned American or European Christian to propagate the Gospel around the world. They have led the way, and it's not time for them to quit, but it may just be time for them to move over and let somebody else do the driving for a while.

One thing for sure is that the Bible does give an example of how missions work should be done, and it is my hope that this manual will present a clear presentation of that Biblical pattern of missions. Hopefully, many churches will choose to follow the example and reshape their church's missions program based upon it. Why is this so important? Let me attempt to explain.

When a church loses its pastor and seeks to hire a replacement, the members generally form what is called a pulpit committee—a group of mature men and/or women in the church—who begin to look over names of possible pastoral candidates. They may target a man who is currently not pastoring or try to entice a man from another church to pastor theirs. Whichever the case may be, the pulpit committee members will look at resumes to judge experience; they will go to hear the man preach, and ultimately, they will ask him to preach to their congregation. Quite possibly, the pulpit committee may consider as few as three or as many as twenty other candidates so the church members can make an informed choice. A pulpit committee goes to great lengths to find the right man and usually has a list of qualifications and criteria for him to meet such as being in a certain age bracket, a height and weight range, as well as having a wife who can play the piano because surely, everyone knows that a pastor's wife, by law, must be able to play the piano. He will be expected to have children and teenagers (so that he can have an outreach to the kids and identify with their parents).

Basically, the same process is followed when hiring a youth pastor. No church ever consults an old folks' home when seeking a youth pastor; the pulpit committee generally hires a candidate who is fresh out of college—still a youth, but one with experience, zeal, a burden, and leadership abilities. Those who are chosen for these important positions must have the proper qualifications. If a church is going to hire an evangelist or an evangelism director, they don't announce in church on a Sunday morning, "Hey, who wants this job?" Of course not! They look for a person who is known in their church, or in their area, or at least known as someone who is extremely gifted in evangelism, energetic toward it, and capable of teaching and motivating others to do the same.

Churches seemingly have criteria for everything they do, except for supporting missionaries. When looking for a missionary to support, about the greatest depth of inquiry made is, "What school did he attend?" A rifled approach is used to find a pastor, an assistant pastor, a financial pastor, a youth pastor, a children's pastor, ad infinitum. But when it comes to supporting missionaries, a shotgun approach is used. Just pull the trigger, and whoever is hit receives support; whoever is missed doesn't receive support. It doesn't matter if one man is 20 and the other is 40, or if one has started 15 churches and the other has only taught a Sunday school class in his last year in Bible college. It doesn't matter if one of them is married with children and the other is single. None of these qualifications seem to matter.

Whether or not the missionary candidate has a knowledge of Scripture, any experience, an ability to speak the language, or an ability to train and teach matters little. None of these logical, Biblical, even minimal attributes matters. All that matters is that the church needs to take on some new missionaries merely because there is enough money in the missions budget to support them. Chances are the next three missionaries who happen to send a request to that church are the three missionaries who will be taken on for support—unless of course a request comes from Sister Josephine's missionary nephew or the son of Brother and Sister Talksalot who recently joined the church and are good tithers. Technically, I don't know if Sister Josephine's nephew can be called a missionary just because he teaches school in another country—English classes, she claims. On the other hand, logic says he must be a missionary because he's in another country, plus his wife works at the home that rears the children of the missionaries for a ten-country region of Africa, so the kids can grow up "normal" with other American children rather than around the "natives." So the church will vote to support Sister Josephine's nephew; after all, she is a good member, faithfully gives to the missions program, and helps out with the building fund.

Do you see my point? Scant care and attention is given to looking for qualified, experienced men to be missionaries, and that is exactly why our children do not aspire to being missionaries and the Great Commission has become the Great Omission.

As you read through these pages, I hope they will be humorous and enjoyable, but I also hope that your eyes will be opened and that you can begin to examine your church's policy on supporting a missionary or on continuing support for a certain missionary. Ask some pertinent questions.

- Where have we gone wrong?
- How can we adjust, adapt, and change what we have been doing in order to become more effective as a church, as families in the church, and as individuals in the family?
- How can we be more effective in fulfilling and helping to fulfill the Great Commission, which Christ gave not just to the church, but to each and every individual Christian?
- How can we help everyone to see that the Great Commission is a mandate for each Christian to fulfill his part in the overall plan of getting the Gospel to everyone alive on the earth in his generation? It can be done, and it will be done—with or without your help.

In the late twentieth century, when the United States government bailed out Chrysler, a new man named Lee Iaccoca took the helm of the company and brought it from bankruptcy to prosperity during the time he was in charge. I well remember the television commercials that Chrysler produced during that time in an attempt to highlight the company's merits to the American buying public. "Here's the guy that's going to take the reins, lead us into prosperity, and help you, the American tax-payer, get you your money back." And he did. What was the slogan that Lee Iacocca used? He stated emphatically, "Either lead, follow, or get out of the way."

I apply that same reasoning to missions today. When I was growing up, I often heard the expression, "If it ain't broke, don't fix it." Correct grammar aside (give me a break, I was born and reared in Georgia, just next door to Alabama), there's a great deal of wisdom in that statement.

On the other side of the coin, I say, "If it is broke, by all means fix it." It is time to stop ignoring the problems, pretend-ing they don't exist, and fearing that someone might actually shine light on the spot of dirt that people already see anyway, but about which no one is doing anything. Iacocca was right, and I intend to apply his logic to my world—the world of mis-sions. It is my hope that these pages will provide the reader with an understanding of what can make an effective missions program in his church and that together we can fix what is bro-ken to the glory of God and for the salvation of the souls for whom His Son gave His life.

Photo: Seen in the back are those who became national church planters, Javong and his wife (both deceased) and Nykaw and Paulu. In the foreground are the Akha ladies singing songs their tribe wrote to honor the Creator Whom they call *Guishaw*. This photo was taken less than a year after their conversion.

[Photo taken June 1987]

UNIT

1

Examining
the
Failure

D id you ever stop to think about the total funds given for missions and what they accomplish? One scale used by missiologists is to divide the reported missionary support for a given nation by the number of converts baptized that year. The following are some examples given by the US Center for World Missions (as well as the *World Christian Encyclopedia*) for the year of 2006. According to their research, Mozambique was the most cost effective nation in that it only required $1,400 of missions funding per baptism.

Mozambique. . . . . . $1,400 (Least expensive)
Ethiopia $2,700 (2nd)
Nepal $3,700 (5th)
Cambodia $4,300 (8th)
Africa $14,000
Asia $61,000
Latin America $145,000
Oceania $634,000
Europe $933,000
United States $1,500,000

How much did it cost per baptism for Final Frontiers in 2006? Just $39.64! That means Final Frontiers results were 35 times more cost effective than the most cost-effective country reporting. Why is Final Frontiers so much more effective? Simple, because Final Frontiers funds church planters only, and to be funded, he must be a soul winner.

Introduction

*Did you know that there are an esti-
mated 3,500 new churches being
started every week throughout the
world?*

Biblically defining the terms *missions*, *missionary*, and *mission field* is the challenge. Without a precise, Biblical understanding of each term, then how can the Great Commission which relies on them possibly be fulfilled?

Did you know that 40 percent of the church's foreign missions resources are being used in just ten "over-saturated" countries which already have successful, nationally run home ministries.

CHAPTER 1

What Is Missions?

Did you know that 28,000 people are being saved each day in China and approximately 20,000 each day in Africa?

For the most part, Christians today do not have a correct understanding of the word *missions*. It is a bit difficult to explain the term without crossing over to the other two of the "triplets" which will be addressed in this section:

- What is a missionary?
- What is a mission field?

But let me give it a try.

When the Great Commission was given, it was fully understood by those who heard it. These people had spent many years with Christ, they had finally come to understand Who He was, and they understood what His plan for the ages was. That plan was unfolded before their eyes, and they were delighted that His plans included them. All they had to do was obey. I believe that His plan was also understood from a cultural standpoint as well.

Let me explain. If you are from Georgia, as I am, and someone challenges you to climb a mountain, then before you is the goal of ascending maybe 2,000 feet to reach the summit of Georgia's highest mountain. But if you are from Southern California or Colorado and are so challenged, you have a much, much higher summit to reach. To accomplish this challenge in Georgia, you need only an hour or two and tennis shoes. To accomplish the goal in Colorado, you need a day or two, climbing gear, hiking gear, ropes, chalk, food, water, etc. For someone living in France who hears of this challenge, it is almost impossible to comprehend as he would have no experience to relate to the challenge. To someone who is a native Floridian, the concept is quite foreign as well since the highest point in Florida is NASA's launch pads; Floridians might even have to consult a dictionary—just to see what a *mountain* is!

When Christ sent His followers into all the world, His commission could have been interpreted in one of two ways. First, they could have interpreted His command as the "Roman world." This limitation would not seem strange to them because it was the only world they knew personally. Remember, in Luke Chapter 2 Caesar Augustus had sent out a decree *"that all the world should be taxed."* Does that mean he taxed Persia, India, and China? All of these lands were known to the Romans, and they even had trade relations with them. But no, "the world" to which Caesar Augustus referred was the world of Roman influence, domination, and control.

It may be that, at first, some of His disciples did interpret His instructions in this way since their journeys show they did not move beyond that realm. Thomas was perhaps the only one who made it outside the dominion of the Roman Empire when he traveled to India, where he allegedly planted seven churches. However, James, our Lord's physical brother, never even left Jerusalem.

The other possible interpretation that they could have received was to literally go into all the earth—even to those regions they did not yet know existed—with the message of the Good News of forgiveness, redemption, atonement, justification, and salvation. Christianity has predominantly held that interpretation.

I submit to you that both views are correct, and at the same time, both are incorrect. The "going," though that is what drives missions, was not the point. The point was in where to go, not in the going. Nor was it limited to these few men as many have since taught for there is no way a handful of men could accomplish that task. It was never Christ's intention to reach nations as they are defined today. God is not so concerned with "Japan," "Kenya," or "Brazil" as He is with those *living* in Japan, Kenya, or Brazil. He did not send His Son to die for geopolitical boundaries on an ever-changing world map. He did send Him to die for those living within those boundaries. However, that is a highly simplified explanation of what He commanded, commissioned, and constructed.

By taking the time to look at what He said, one can know precisely what He meant. When I was growing up, I can recall my father's speaking to me in real-estate terms saying, "Before you buy the house, check out the neighborhood." His advice still makes sense, and likewise the same should be done in one's Biblical interpretation. Learn not just what He said but also learn what He was saying.

I do not know Greek, so I have to rely upon the knowledge of those who do. But universally, scholars seem to agree that the word nation has absolutely no reference to geographical or geopolitical boundaries. It is instead the Greek word *ethnos*, from which the English word *ethnic* is derived.

The change in today's meaning is relatively new on the stage of world history. Currently, the word *nation* is used interchangeably with the word *country*. Barely a hundred years ago the word *nation* was used to refer to specific ethnic, tribal, or people groups, such as the Cherokee nation and the Sioux nation. Even the classic novel *The Last of the Mohicans* was about an Indian nation...hmmm, now what were they called?

Paul emphasized this fact in Athens when speaking before the Areopagus, the high court/local Mensa chapter as recorded in Acts 17:26, 27, which says, *"And hath made of one blood all nations of men for to dwell on all the face of the earth, and hath determined the times before appointed, and the bounds of their habitation;* [27] *That they should seek the Lord, if haply they might feel after him, and find him, though he be not far from every one of us."*

Paul was saying that God, in ages past, pre-determined the geopolitical and geographical areas where the various ethnic or people groups or tribes would live. God not only determined their location but also the length of time they would be in that location. And that time seems never to be permanent. However, just because a people may be uprooted by conquerors, disease, or natural catastrophes and moved into the others' lands, they do not cease to be a separate, distinct, unique nation or people.

The Jews may be in nearly every country of the world, but they are still Jews. They might claim their nationality is American, but in technical terms, their nationality is Jewish, and they are citizens of America. The same holds true for the Hmong living in Sacramento, the Khmer living in Long Beach, the Koreans living in Augusta, the Vietnamese living in Columbus, the Carib living in New York, and the Honduran living in my house. The word our Lord used when He gave the commission was not to reach *countries*, but to reach *ethnic groups* inhabiting those countries. His purpose was the fulfillment of His prophecy given in Habakkuk 2:14, with the prophet stating a future time when, *"...the earth shall be filled with the knowledge of the glory of the LORD, as the waters cover the sea."*

Have you ever seen a spot in the sea that was not covered by water? From the receding foam on the beach to the deepest depths of the ocean, there is not a single square inch of the sea that is not totally and completely covered by water. My dad told me that when he was in the Navy, an expression was used to illustrate how necessary the individual sailor was compared to the whole. The sailors were told to dip a cup into the sea; then they were informed that the size of the hole the cup made was equal to the amount of their significance. He was also told in paratrooper school that if his chute did not work, he should bring it back, and he would be issued another. Is it any wonder my brothers and I avoided the Navy!

It is not God's singular intention that not just His glory cover the earth because it already does. In fact David stated in Psalm 19:1, *"The heavens declare the glory of God...."* It is His intention and expressed will that the **knowledge** of His glory inundate the earth to the same degree that the flood in Noah's time did. He wants to be glorified by His most precious creation made in His image—mankind. It has never been Satan's desire to turn the stones or the forest or the flowers against God; his only aim has been to turn man against God.

The Bible contains one example after another of God's attempts to woo man back to Him and His message and messenger being resisted, persecuted, ignored, and/or killed, until finally the same became the lot of His only begotten Son, Jesus Christ. But Christ, being man and God, crushed Satan's scheme and annihilated his work by using the sacrifice of His own blood as a purification of our sins. He killed death by embracing it and taking it to the grave; then He left it behind as He arose triumphantly three days later, forever sealing His salvation with the indwelling presence of His Holy Spirit into the lives of all who believe on Him.

Not content to leave that message with the Jews alone, He, the One Who was given power and leave by His Father to speak and the world was created, transferred the use of that power to man. He transferred the use of that power for the express purpose of taking the message of His Father's grace and goodness and glory to the sum total, not of all men, not of all countries, but of all ethnic groups so that from there the message would filter down into every clan and every family until finally, His goal of total global emersion in the knowledge of God's glory would be accomplished.

Christ then jump-started the process at Pentecost. All those who heard the Gospel there were, for the most part, Jews from other lands though some were no doubt Gentile converts as well as tourists and businessmen looking to gain a huge profit. This can be deduced because more than a dozen ethnic groups were listed as being present who heard the marvelous works of God in their own languages.

Having begun the process, it was continued day after day throughout the city of Jerusalem until everyone had heard it. Then the message was carried to Samaria and the outer regions of Syria, to Damascus, to Antioch, then westward all the way to England. From there, like the ball in a Pong game, it bounced back into the heart of Europe and on to the Orient. Even misguided, doctrinally lethal monks carried it to the shores of the New World. Their doctrine may have been wrong, but they understood the commission. After all these centuries, doctrinal truth is choking out the doctrinal errors as more and more Latinos come to the truth of God's Word and learn that our Advocate is not the mother of Christ, but Christ Himself.

Today, Latin missionaries have begun retracing the course that brought the Gospel to them and are going as missionaries to the Middle East, Asia, and India. And now, even before the dawn of a new century, every country on earth has heard the Gospel. Barriers that could not be broken by man have been smashed by the Internet and radio. Within a generation, every existing ethnic group on the planet will have heard the Gospel. Can it be done? You bet it can! It can be done, and the truth is, it is being done by those who are leading while others follow their lead.

Those who think the task is too great are ignorant of what God is already doing around the world. Armies of unnamed and unknown national missionaries are skirmishing daily against the forces of Satan all around the earth. Those who listen can hear the gates of Hell falling before their aggressive advance in villages and cities everywhere. The awesome power our Lord willed to us as He ascended into Heaven is being tapped and is transforming the landscape. Technological growth in the use of computer and sciences such as demographics have helped to locate the last remaining ethnic groups that have yet to hear the Gospel. Once located and targeted, the nearest missionary

is found who either speaks their language; or speaks a somewhat similar, understandable language; or at worst, a foreign
missionary can be sent to learn their language, then lead them
to the Light.

I say it that way because I am time-driven, not only in my
own life, but for the lives of those who are dying without Christ.
Obviously, a man who speaks Spanish can pick up Portuguese
much more quickly than a man who speaks only Swahili or
English. It is better to find someone who lives nearby and
speaks a similarly rooted language than to take the time to send
an outsider. It may take the foreign missionary five or ten years
to become proficient enough to witness while it takes an indigenous person five or six months.

So lastly and finally, how are these unreached ethnic groups
found and then won to Christ?

This planet, at least in missionary terms, has been divided
into what is called "The Three Worlds": World A, World B, and
you guessed it—World C. Allow me to define them:

World A

- The truly **"unreached world"** of people who have never
  even heard the name of Jesus.
- Percentage of global population: 28 percent
- Percentage of missionaries targeting World A: 2.5 percent

World B

- The **"unevangelized world"** of people who have limited
  access to the Gospel but are not yet considered "Christian" nations. The Gospel has penetrated their borders
  but has not reached the majority of the people. Given
  time, the majority of the people will be reached—perhaps
  within two or three generations.
- Percentage of global population: 39 percent
- Percentage of missionaries targeting World B: 17.5 percent

World C

- The **"evangelized world"** of people who have full and unrestricted access to the Gospel, regardless of whether or not they choose to hear or accept it
- Percentage of global population: 33 percent
- Percentage of missionaries targeting World C: 80 percent

Did you digest all of these facts and figures? Good, but let me point out that in any given location or country, people groups (tribes or ethnos) can make up one or more segments. For example, the Philippines have great exposure to the Gospel, and they are part of World B. However, tribes on some of their 7,000+ islands are still classified as "World A" because they have never heard of Jesus and ethnically are not Filipinos. The people have a separate language and culture different from all other inhabitants of the Philippines. These tribes must be found and exposed to the Gospel.

I am convinced that in every culture, and I mean every one of them, that there are cultural keys which will unlock the door for the Gospel to rush in. (In fact, I am now starting to write a book on this subject, giving illustrations from tribes and nations from all over the world). For now, let me share just one illustration which, by the way, was the single event that launched Final Frontiers.

In September 1986 I took a missions trip to the country of Thailand to visit Tommy Tillman, the man who had trained me for the ministry when I was a teenager. At that time he had a ministry to the lepers. Today he not only works in Thailand but also in Mongolia. Tommy Tillman is truly a modern-day Paul.

I was traveling to Thailand to make a video presentation that I could take to churches to raise support for him so that he could remain in Thailand doing ministry rather than having to return stateside continuously to raise more funds. In 1986 video was still primarily an industrial tool, but thankfully, I had friends who worked in Hollywood, loved the Lord, and were willing to help me with the project. I had been given the name and phone number of a retired schoolteacher from New Mexico named Charlie Holmes, who had visited Thailand several years earlier where he met a missionary from the Philippines who used English classes as a method of planting churches. They had fallen in love and married. I had never before met Charlie or Lourdes, but during the phone conversation, they invited me to leave with them the following morning to visit some "national preachers" in the "hill tribe" area of northern Thailand.

I was intrigued by their invitation. I didn't know what a national preacher was; in fact, I don't think I had ever heard the term. Equally strange to me was the term "hill tribes." I didn't know what to expect, but a train ride north to the cooler mountains to scout out some good scenes for the video sounded too good to pass up. I settled into the bed for a good night's sleep, not knowing that within 24 hours my life would totally change. In fact, what I was about to see and experience affected me so deeply that when I returned home, my wife, from a personality viewpoint, no longer recognized me. I was about to discover my destiny and to be baptized into the reality of why God had caused me to be born.

Those who know me and know Final Frontiers know that serving national preachers is my purpose in life, but at that moment in 1986, I had never heard the term and did not know what it meant. Curiosity seized me, and I made arrangements to travel with them later that week to the northern city of Chiang Mai, a quaint, walled city that was an ancient capital of Siam as well as home to the first Thai convert, who was subsequently burned alive after his conversion. Now, 25 years after I first arrived there, Chiang Mai is a bustling, polluted business center of more than 2 million inhabitants and probably the number-one tourist spot in Thailand. Its hot weather is much milder than Bangkok's, and for that reason, 80 percent of all missionaries in Thailand live there.

Let those figures sink into your mind for a moment. In a

country of nearly 60 million souls (at that time), 80 percent of all the missionaries lived in a city of only 2 million. I hate to be sarcastic (and I certainly don't know the mind of God), but I find it incredibly interesting how God seems to almost always call missionaries to serve in the places that are the most comfortable. Frankly, I think God gets blamed for much that should be blamed on basic human desire. But I digress.

Looking back, I don't remember if we traveled by bus or by train, but I do remember that after arriving, I was introduced to Samuel Mani (pronounced Sam-well), his brother-in-law Jimmy Tachinam, and their friend Luke Bee. These names of course, are all westernized, adopted names. I never thought to ask for the real names of Samuel and Jimmy, but I discovered that Luke's real name is Boonroat Premsanjaint. Saying "Luke" is much easier, wouldn't you agree? He is from the Lisu tribe (or nation). Samuel and Jimmy were both Rawang from northern Burma, now called Myanmar. They were both sons-in-law of a preacher named Javong, who was from the Lahushi Tribe.

Jimmy was extremely musical and had taught his converts to sing in four-part harmony. He spent a great deal of time translating songs from English or his native tongue into the languages of the tribes to whom he ministered. He spoke nearly ten languages. Samuel was fluent in a dozen languages and also knew Hebrew and Greek. All three of these men had shortwave radio broadcasts over FEBC short-wave radio in multiple languages, with over 300,000 listeners in Thailand, Burma, Laos, Vietnam, and China.

Upon arriving in Chiang Mai and meeting these men, I said goodbye to Charlie and Lourdes and left with Samuel, Jimmy, and Luke to travel further north into the Golden Triangle to the region of Chiengrai. On the journey, I was able to get to know these men better by listening to their stories and ministry experiences. They had all been serving God for more than 20 years and were a bit older than me. Samuel and Jimmy were from a region in northern Burma where China and Tibet meet.

This area was known during World War II as "the hump." Many pilots were shot down there and never found due to the dense jungles. Most of their tribe were Christians and had a healthy missionary spirit. As young men, they had volunteered to give their lives to the tribes living south of them. Their ministries were primarily among the Lisu, Lahu, and Akha tribes. They had lived there for so long that they were as one with the tribes and had married Javong's daughters.

All of their languages were from the same root language, so learning additional languages was like a native Spanish person learning French or Italian. For them, it was easy. Most of these languages, however, did not have a written script at that time, so they had adopted what was known as the "Fraser script"[1] to teach the people their respective alphabets. After evangelizing a village, their method was to teach them to read their own spoken language and then to translate songs and Bible portions for them. At this time the Akha tribe did not have a single page of the Bible of which they were aware in their own language.

Enroute to Chiengrai, we passed through an area called Mae Suay which they had begun to evangelize. Just a short walking distance from the main road and situated on top of a hill was a village that would later become known as Zion Hill. To me, it became holy ground.

At the bottom of the hill we had to abandon our truck and begin walking. All I could see at the time was tall grass and the tops of bamboo huts on distant hills. Soon I could see people walking about in colorful costumes, but we were still too far

---

[1]James O'Fraser (1886-1938) was a Scottish missionary who worked with the China Inland Mission among the Lisu tribe of China. He had used the letters of the English alphabet and assigned the tonal pronunciation of the Lisu language to create the letters of their alphabet. The individual English letters (in appearance) became the Lisu langage in pronunciation. Because their language has more sounds than English, in some cases a letter might appear as an upside down "A." This became a common practice for linguists to use as they evangelized other tribes in the region, and the Fraser script is still currently in use.

away to make out any detail. My heart was beating wildly, not from the walk, but because of what I was seeing. As we reached the summit, we passed some idols lying on the ground on both sides of the trail and a few totems that marked the boundary of the village. "Outside" the village gate where we were was the domain of the spirits. The totems served to identify the boundaries between the spirit world and the human world and to serve as a sort of "scarecrow" to keep out the evil spirits.

Within a moment, we were walking along a well-worn trail that passed bamboo huts, most of which were open on one side. Chickens ran across the path in front of us followed by pot-bellied pigs. Dogs tied by cords to the posts of the elevated huts barked wildly, showing their teeth. I began to see people looking at us through the cracks of their bamboo huts. Children began to cry as women were screaming and calling out to their neighbors. They would run out of their houses, grab their children like an eagle in flight grabbing its prey, and then run to hide. Men, dressed in what looked like black pajamas, began to scurry out of the houses and up the trails winding up from the rice patties below us.

Soon they were approaching me with their long knives in hand that they used to harvest their rice crops. Jimmy and Samuel said something to them in their language, and they seemed to stop in their tracks. I looked around me in amazement. I had never seen anything happen like this in my life. It was as if I had stepped back in time.

When I was a child in Atlanta, I would lie on my back in the grass and watch the planes fly overhead, wondering where they were headed and what it was like in distant lands. I would read stories of explorers and missionaries and lament that there were no "undiscovered" civilizations left to find. But at this moment, I knew I had been wrong. I had stepped into a world so primitive that words could barely describe it, but if you keep reading, you'll get the picture.

For a moment in time I was frozen on that hillside, wondering if I was about to be invited to a feast—not as a guest of honor—but as the main course! Something in the words of my friends had caused the men to halt while tightly gripping their long knives in their hands. The sensation of threat seemed to have passed, and their expressions turned to curiosity.

Jimmy looked at me and, in his broken English, told me to preach to them, and he would translate. When I opened my Bible and spoke my first words, the men jumped back in horror, but their wonder held them captive. They stood as I began to tell them about the streets of gold in Heaven. "What?!"

As a preacher, I'll let you in on a little secret? Sometimes when we are preaching, we are also having a conversation in our minds with ourselves saying things like, "What did I just say?" or "I have to hurry up!" While you are hearing us declare God's Word, we can actually be thinking about something else. I say that to explain that as I was talking to them about the streets of gold, I was thinking to myself, "Jonny, what are you doing? These people have no idea about Heaven or Jesus or anything, and you idiot, for their first exposure to the Word of God, you are talking about streets of gold!" But since I had already begun, I had to finish.

Surprisingly, my listeners seemed interested and began to move closer to me until I was finally surrounded and those in the back could not see me, even though I towered over them in height. Jimmy stopped me and suggested we take the "service" into a hut a few yards away. The room, which was about 20 feet by 50 feet was quickly filled to capacity, and those who could not enter stood outside looking through the window openings and doorway. The roof was made of long grass and palm branches, and the walls were constructed of woven bamboo. The floor was made of woven bamboo as well. As I shifted my weight from foot to foot, I would slip through the cracks and stumble, but their obvious interest kept me going. I progressed in subject from the streets of gold to the Creation, to the fall of man, to atonement in the Old Testament, to the perfect and complete sacrifice of Christ in the New Testament, to His coming again to take us to Heaven where there are (yes, you guessed it!) streets of gold.

It was probably mid-afternoon when we had arrived in the village, and I preached to them until about 2:00 a.m. In the crowd were both Akha and Lahu as two Lahu villages were nearby, and somehow the word had spread to them about our arrival. Their curiosity had brought them to see us. Therefore, every sentence had to be translated into two languages. The two languages, though from a common root, are still quite different in their delivery. A paragraph in English translates to what seems like a single sentence in Lahu; but for the Akha, one paragraph in English seems to become an entire book in their language! Now you can understand why it took so long to teach them.

Finally, I told Samuel that I was too tired to continue. The four of us were then led by some men to a nearby house with a porch about eight feet off the ground. A notched, slanted pole leading from the ground to the porch served as a ladder. We climbed up the pole one by one, putting one foot in front of the other (I must have looked like a beach ball climbing up a straw), and we were followed by a number of the elders of the village, as well as some other tribal preachers who had come to meet us. They wanted to know more about me. We entered the central room of the hut where some candles were lit so we could see.

Akha houses typically have a central room that serves as a gathering place and kitchen, a room to one side where the females and young children sleep, and sometimes a room to the other side where the males sleep. These rooms are divided by a bamboo curtain. As I sat listening to the elders and the preachers chatter, I had to wonder about the wisdom of using candles in a dried-out, bamboo/grass hut!

After a few moments, some ladies climbed the ladder and brought in food—pineapple, mangos, small Asian bananas and what they affectionately call "sticky rice" for us on rattan platters. One by one each man would reach into the pot of rice, and pull out a plug of it, dip it into some sauce made from hot, black peppers, among other ingredients, and then place it in his mouth. No one had washed. In fact, the Akha did not wash. They had no soap, no shampoo—nothing with which to clean. They also had no toilet paper as that was evidently why God created the left hand. They did however have an abundance of lice, dirt, filth, and communal drinking and eating utensils. But I really didn't mind. It was part of the adventure. To be honest, the food was excellent and revived me a bit.

I remember thinking that the mushrooms I was eating were the juiciest I had ever had. When I commented on them, I was told that they were not mushrooms; they were leeches. I decided that I would skip the rest of my salad and go directly to the diced steak which I found well-cooked and spicy. I wondered how they had such good steak in the middle of nowhere. Then I was told that it was not steak; it was dog. I have to admit it was good.

Years later my wife and children would happily feast on the same meal in the same village. We have enjoyed dog meat ever since. Even today we have three running around the house. No, don't worry, they are pets! (Besides, Chihuahuas are only good as a tasty appetizer.)

As we ate, we began to get to know each other better. I asked them why they had acted so afraid of me when I had first entered their village. They told me that they had never before seen a white man and did not know they existed. They thought I was an albino monkey, and they had come to kill and eat me. When I started speaking, they became really terrified. They wanted to know where I was from, so I told them "America," to which they responded, "Where is that village?"

"It is on the other side of the world," I answered.

They huddled together for a moment, and then one asked, "How do you keep from falling off?"

I feebly explained, "The world is round," and they politely

accepted my reasoning, though I had to wonder if they really believed me.

One elderly man asked, "How long did it take you to get here?"

I replied, "About three days."

"Why so long?" he asked.

"It took a long time because I had to cross the ocean."

Then he asked, "What is an ocean?"

By now I fully understood that they did not fully understand my terms, so I tried to explain it in a way they could follow. "The ocean is a really wide river," I ventured.

He responded, "How did you cross such a wide river?"

When I started to tell them I flew, I realized that I would shock them beyond belief, and they might want to throw me off the porch—just to see if I could in fact fly! Instead I quickly changed the subject by asking, "When I came here today, at first you were all afraid of me. Suddenly your fear turned to curiosity. Why?"

They responded that my mention of the streets of gold calmed them.

"Why?" was my logical question.

Their incredible answer still rings in my head today. One of the elder men spoke up and said, "Years ago all men lived in one village and worshipped the Creator."

I interrupted the beginning of the narrative to ask if they knew the name of the village, and they did. In their language it was called "the village where the mustards grow."[2]

He continued, "We all lived there together as one people until we began to displease the Creator. He came down from the skies, and in His anger, divided us into different groups and gave each group its own language. That is where the different tribes come from. Then He made us separate from each other

---

[2]The Bible tells of such a city called Babel located on the plain of Shinar. Incredibly, the word *shinar* in its original language means "mustard."

and gave to each tribe a book about Himself in their own, new language."[3]

I interrupted again to ask if they had that book. With such an archaeological find, I believe I could have financed the evangelization of the entire world. Sadly, they responded that they did not. They said that their forefathers were careless with it and when they saw the other tribes losing their books, they decided to eat the book so that the words of the Creator would be inside them, and their people would never lose contact with Him. Since that time they had lost the knowledge of the Creator. Then one of the elders spoke up and said, "That is why we call ourselves Akha."

"Why? What does *Akha* mean?" I asked.

He responded, "It means 'stupid.'"

I sat in amazement, momentarily pondering his reply. In our culture, if a man has no knowledge of God or denies His existence, he's considered intelligent, and he is called "Professor." In their society, losing the knowledge of God meant they were "stupid."

"Which of our cultures," I wondered, "is really the primitive one?"

As he continued his history lesson, he went on to say that since they had lost their book, they had drifted further and further away from God (whom they call *Guishaw*) and had become enslaved to the demon spirits. Their tribal legend, however, told them that someday, someone would again bring them the book about the Creator, and it would tell about the village where He lives and where all the paths are made of gold. He concluded, "When you began to tell us today about the paths of gold, we knew the Book had finally come to us once again."

---

[1]The Lisu said their book was made from rice paper, and during a famine they ate it. Since then they have lost the knowledge of the Creator. The Lahu said theirs was written on leather, and their forefathers carelessly allowed dogs to take it. The dogs tore it to pieces, so since that time, they have been without the Book.

I was astonished at what I had just heard. Then I began to understand that I had been allowed by God to be the messenger to bring back the Word of God to these people who had been without it since the Tower of Babel. Countless generations of their tribesmen had entered eternity without the Book and without the Saviour. Never had I dreamed that I would be used in such a way. It was the greatest honor of my life! Now I felt I had the task of ensuring that every Akha alive would be able to know that "the Word" had come. This experience changed my life forever.

It was interesting to hear some of the glimpses of truth that they had retained which had been polluted over time. They knew of Heaven, and they knew of Hell. Their salvation was, in fact, dependent on their eldest son. Let me explain. When a father died, the family sacrificed a water buffalo, and at that time the oldest son had to quote the father's entire genealogy as well as all the villages lived in back to the first Akha. They believe the first Akha to be the first man, Adam. The son has to be able to quote each one, and it is incredible that any of them can actually quote their generations considering they are "slash-and-burn" farmers who move every few years after the soil nutrients are depleted, and a man can live in a dozen villages in his lifetime.

Once the quotation is complete, if the son remembered successfully, the spirit of the dead father will ride the spirit of the slain buffalo into Heaven. If the son was not successful, Hell would be the home for his deceased father. Salvation was dependent on his eldest son; just as our salvation is dependent on our "elder Brother," Jesus Christ. The journey takes place in a casket hewn from forest trees which resembles a boat. The Akha are notably fearful of rivers and only go near to draw water. Yet they are "saved" if you will, by a boat—just as Noah was.

You may remember that I mentioned the villagers had a gate at the entrance of their villages. A person is only safe from the evil spirits when he enters the gate. Inside the gate his salvation is provided by his eldest son. A strange belief, considering that the "eldest" Son of God is also man's gate (or door) to Heaven. Many such analogies or perversions of Truth exist in their legends and customs as in all others around the world. Finding and explaining the truth of them opens the door to witnessing. But again, I digress.

After some time I began to shift my conversation to the tribal preachers who had also met us that day, in order to find out about their ministries. I learned that each of them pastored three, five, or even seven churches and, in addition, had to toil all day in the hot sun, growing rice for their family to eat and flax or hemp for their wives to make their clothing on home-made bamboo looms.

My plan had been to raise funds for my missionary friend, thinking $1,000 a month would keep him on the field, and he would not have to come home on furlough. I began to wonder if it would not be better to give the money to these men who could reach those whom my friend could not. After all, as an American missionary, he could raise all the support he wanted by his own efforts, but who would speak for these servants of God?

Through the interpreter I asked if they could live with $1,000 a month. I wondered if such an amount would be sufficient for each of these men. They huddled together for a moment and then one asked, "What does that mean, $1,000?" I had not realized they lived in a society that did not use money. They bartered for all they had. The people had no concept at all of how much money $1,000 was. We began to discuss their needs for food, clothing, etc., and determined that in order for them to leave the rice patties and be full-time in the ministry, they each needed only $1 a day!

When I returned to my church, I took the message that for one dollar a day a national pastor would have all the support he needed. As of this writing, nearly 1,400 such men in 84 countries have collectively started over 36,000 churches. These churches average between 30 and 40 new converts upon inception. All are documented for those who may doubt such a miracle.

Many times in many villages, this same scenario has been repeated over and over—not by me—but by the preachers and students who were trained at Zion Hill. I have visited many villages that no longer have totems or spirit shelves; instead, they have a church! And if they know visitors are coming, they will line both sides of the trail and hang strings of flowers around the visitors' neck as they sing songs of praise to the Lord Jesus which were written or taught by Jimmy. Sometimes they even make up their own songs praising God for making their rice to grow and for chasing the rats from their fields (which by the way travel in packs and grow to the size of a dog). They sing songs praising God for the rain that washes them and for the Book that has once again come to them. These people sing from their hearts. They don't know as much theology as Americans do, but they do more with what they know than can be imagined.

I have stayed at and around Zion Hill many times since then, either with my family or away from them for weeks at a time. I even contracted typhoid there several years later. The structure in which the first service was held ultimately became a classroom and later a dining hall for the Bible college that was begun. The house where we met and slept in became the men's dormitory. Many times in many such villages, I, like Robert Moffat, the famous Scottish missionary to Africa, would step out on the porch at night and look out over the valley and hilltops, only to see the campfires of scores of villages still waiting to hear that the Book has come.

Today if you were to visit Zion Hill with me, the grave of Jimmy Tachinam is at the very spot where I first opened the Book to preach. He is no longer with the people; he is probably dancing along the streets of gold—no doubt teaching the angels to sing in four-part harmony! With him is Javong and his wife;

the wife of Paulu, our first Akha pastor; A-Ju and his wife; A-So; and so many others. At their funerals, no buffalo were slain because they and all their people knew that Christ was their sacrifice, slain for their sin.

Today I am told that over 95 percent of the Akha villages in Thailand are now considered to be Christian. These people are taking the Gospel to their brethren in Laos, Myanmar, China, and Vietnam. Preachers still walk the jungle trails, dodging the tigers on land and the crocodiles in the rivers. These preachers cross national borders like we cross a city street and go where no American missionary can go. These men of God are doing it with no money in their pockets, no health insurance, no IRAs, and no pension. They do not travel in planes or on buses or trains; they walk. They don't sleep in hotels; they sleep on the ground or on dirt floors. They eat whatever is provided for them by the villages where they enter as the first messenger of the Gospel ever to venture there. Often they are hungry, wet, and persecuted, but they continue on.

- **Their goal?** For all their "cousins" to hear the Gospel.
- **Their vision?** To win souls and start churches.
- **Their hope?** That some way, somehow, someday, someone will step forward with a dollar a day for them to feed their families while they are busy in the Master's vineyard.

That too is my hope, and to that end, I have labored for the past 25 years. That is why there is an organization called Final Frontiers. I am thankful for all those who have helped, and I am likewise ashamed for all those who could have and should have but did not. How much of what you have amassed in the past 25 years will you carry with you into eternity? Currently I have nearly 400 preachers on a waiting list who are still serving while they wait for sponsorship, and some are even dying while they wait for someone to help them be more effective servants of God.

Currently, a number of faithful, elderly Akha, Lahu, and Lisu preachers remain in that region, as well as those of other tribes. Among them is Cainan, who lives in China. When his support began in 1986, he had already served for 40 years without receiving one penny of support. Many of these preachers who are in their forties today were only young teenagers when I met them. Some were among those who first stood around me as I talked about the streets of gold. All are faithfully preaching where Americans cannot and living in a manner that most Americans would not. I would personally appreciate any assistance to help them reach every member of their tribe for Christ.

I trust that these illustrations convincingly show what missions really is. It is not building churches; it is planting churches. Everything else is ministry, but it is not missions. Of course, the temptation is to say that if one is doing support work for the missionaries, then he is in effect, a missionary. I will spend the next pages of this book trying to convince you otherwise, but not for the purpose of belittling anyone's ministry; rather, I wish to set the record straight. Missions is broken, and in refusing to admit it, to see it, or to discuss the possibility of it, then how will it ever be fixed?

Does being employed by the Atlanta Falcons, as every football player surely wishes he were, make him a football player? No! Because the employee might be a bus driver, a water boy, a coach, an assistant coach, the general manager, a secretary, or even the owner. While each employee is involved in the business of football and each one draws a paycheck from the same account, only those who are gifted, proven, experienced, and set apart as a player are allowed to wear the uniform, take the field, cash a big check, and call themselves a football player. The coach's job is important and so is that of the water boy, but they are not players and should not be called players. They are *ministers* (which means "servants") to the players, helping them better do what they are gifted and trained to do. Ministers are needed on the field; they should be called what they are because they deserve the title and the honor that goes with it.

CHAPTER 2

What Is a Missionary?

*Did you know that in 100 A.D. there
was 1 congregation for every 12 unreached people groups? Today there
are more than 416 congregations for
each unreached people group!*

How Can a Person Be a Missionary
if He Does Not Know What the Term Means?

Missions, and by association, *missionary* and *mission field*, are perhaps the most misunderstood-under-standable terms in modern Christianity.

Lester Roloff, a marvelous pastor and evangelist of past years, operated a broad ministry to troubled youth and salvaged many lives with the help of his staff. He flew a plane which was ultimately his undoing and weekly took teenage boys and girls into churches across American to sing, quote Scripture, and help him raise the needed funding for his ministry. Operating the Roloff homes required more than his individual church could provide.

Lester Roloff never referred to himself as a missionary. He was addressed as "Pastor Roloff," "Evangelist Roloff," "Dr. Roloff," and "Brother Roloff" but never as "Missionary Roloff." Why not? Quite simply, Lester Roloff was not a missionary. Yet his not being a missionary per se did not deter or limit his ministry or fundraising. I imagine if Dr. Roloff was alive today, he would be called "Missionary Roloff," which would most certainly confuse his church members in Corpus Christi, Texas, since they paid his salary and he preached in their pulpit weekly. It is amazing that he never expressed any regret or insult over not being called a missionary. Could it be that he was proud of and satisfied with the calling God had given him?

For centuries the definition of a missionary has been both obvious and definite. Only in the last few decades of the twentieth century has the definition morphed to become whatever anyone wants to do outside of local church employment as far as ministry is concerned and to make a living at doing it. In other words, those currently doing ministry not directly linked to a local church now present themselves with the title of "missionary." Career ministry servants who in past days provided support functions such as teachers, airplane mechanics, boarding school attendants, and so forth, have now become "missionaries" by our current, cultural, but not Biblical definition.

Competent men who pastor churches near American military bases refer to themselves as "missionaries to the military"—as if Christian military personnel have no concept of or are either unable or unwilling to tithe or support their own pastor. Quite simply, if a man pastors the military in Fayetteville, North Carolina, he is called "pastor"; if he pastors the military in Frankfurt, Germany, he is called "missionary." They both pastor the same military, with the same rank, living with the same family, learning the same doctrine, tithing off the same salary; but they have different titles. Why is that? The answer is, in the vernacular of our real-estate friends, "location, location, and location." The implication is that though a missionary to the military may be living in a foreign nation, his target group is not the citizens of that land, but rather to the American personnel who live there. Frankly, such illustrations reveal the fact that the term *missionary* has become the most misunderstood-understandable word in modern Christianity.

There was a time when using the word *missions* implied doing missionary work, that is to say planting a church, training a national to take that church over as pastor, then moving on to the next town and repeating the process. But today missions is defined by any number of scenarios, and quite frankly, the word has become so often used and abused that it very seldom has anything to do with doing real, Biblical missionary work—not that any of these other functions are of themselves wrong, evil, or unnecessary. They are perhaps mostly of a worthwhile nature, but they do not a missionary make or require.

Take for example what is commonly referred to as the "rescue mission," often found in the poorer areas of modern cities. They are places of refuge inhabited by men and ladies who have succumbed to and have been overcome by alcohol and drugs. As a result, these "down and outers" lost the normal lives which they previously lived. They come to the rescue mission to be with friends, get instruction and encouragement, get food, get shelter, and hopefully someday, get their lives back. These places are referred to as rescue missions because the goal of the founders or leaders of these missions is to rescue those who are in dire need of such help. So in this sense, the word *mission* can refer to a struggle or a challenge that has been placed before people.

But Biblically speaking in reference to the word *missions*, I am referring to the *work of missionaries*, which is church planting and training others for ministry. For that reason, many people no longer associate doing missionary work with that of being a missionary. For example, today's missions include, but are not limited to, youth missions, missions to the elderly, missions to soup kitchens, and missions which include teaching at Bible colleges, working in orphanages, feeding centers, and even doing mechanical work for missionaries who are pilots. Missions has morphed into any number of venues.

None of these areas of service are in and of themselves

wrong; in fact, they are very worthwhile ministries that need to be done and should be supported. The point is that perhaps what they should be called is "ministries"—not missions. One might wonder if it's such a big deal to go to all the trouble to make a point over the distinction of being called a missionary that someone like me could actually write an entire book about the matter. After all, it's just semantics, or is it?

Allow me to illustrate why I feel the abuse of the term is a doctrinal error that has brought irreparable damage to the cause of Christ. Most of Christianity still operates under the belief that the position of a pastor should be reserved to a man. I am aware that in today's culture, the twenty-first century, that belief offends some. However, rather than being concerned about what is offensive to man, I am more concerned about what is offensive to God; you know, like gluttony, gossip, sowing discord...ooops, I got off point.

Where was I? Oh yes, the Bible says in I Timothy 3:2 that a pastor should be the husband of one wife. Obviously, this Scripture teaches that a woman should not be a pastor because she cannot be the husband of one wife. Does that mean God is anti-feminine? No. Does it mean that women are not capable? No. Does it mean that a woman could not be as good a pastor as a man can be? No. Does it mean that she cannot study the Word of God in as much depth as a man can? No. It simply means that Almighty God, for whatever reasons that were important to Him even if they are no longer important to America's culture, determined that the position of a pastor which He created should be left to a qualified man, not to a woman.

What is the point that I'm trying to make in addressing this issue? Simply that ladies in our Biblically solid churches today are extremely gifted in teaching. Multiplied gifted women are teachers, but they would never be addressed as "Pastor." "Sister Jones" is not called the pastor of the third-grade Sunday school class; she is called the teacher. By the same token, Brother Jones is the teacher of the fifth grade Sunday school class; he is also referred to as a teacher. Why are they not called pastors? After all, they are teaching, and that is what a pastor does. They are also instructing, praying, and taking care of their class members as a shepherd would, but they are not called pastors. Why? Because they are not pastors and because pastors do not like to share the title they have worked so hard to earn with those who have not made the effort to earn that position. Lastly, because they are simply not pastors; they are teachers.

I have children, I love my children, and I am a good parent to my children. However, I can never be my children's mother. I can call myself their mother, and I can even ask them to call me "Mom," but I will still never be their mother.

When my first wife died, I tried to fill the role of both father and mother but failed miserably. I was inadequate to fulfill the challenge before me. Does this mean that a mother loves more than a father? No. Does it mean that a mother cares more than a father? No, it simply means that a man cannot be a mother. He can do the work of a mother, he can be in the place of a mother, but he cannot be a mother.

Many wise, wonderful women have built great ministries. The New Testament lists several including Priscilla, the wife of Aquila, who assisted her husband in training Apollos, one of the leaders of the early Church. No difference is given in Scripture between the influence Priscilla had on Apollos as opposed to the influence Aquila had on him. They were, for all practical purposes and as far as Scripture reveals, equal. Priscilla may have even had a greater influence on him than her husband, but the Scripture does not tell us that. The point is that semantics are important because semantics can change the meaning of a word.

Allow me to share another example. One semantical difference in modern religion is the definition of the term *baptism*. I am a Baptist, and Baptists believe baptism should be done by immersion. Others believe it can be done by sprinkling or by literally placing a drop of water on the convert's head. Some would question whether or not that is a big deal. Well, to those who do not study the Word of God or to those who do not attribute preeminence to or authority in the Word of God, perhaps it is not important. For those who place greater value on culture and/or tradition than Scripture, perhaps it is not important. But for those who seek and yearn for the truth and want to know how something was defined and performed, it makes a world of difference. How can one know what the true way of baptism is?

The answer is very simple—by looking at the language in which the Scripture was written. In doing so, the student will discover that the word for *baptism*, or the verb, *to baptize*, in the Greek language in which the New Testament was written, literally means "to immerse, to dunk, or to make fully wet." That directive can only be accomplished through the form of baptism known as immersion, where someone steps into a pool of water or a river or a lake or an ocean and is literally, totally, 100 percent immersed in the water. Anything else is not literally baptism.

People may call their method baptism. They may want it to be known as baptism. They may change the definition of the verb in order to make it baptism from a modern, cultural viewpoint. But changing their practice will never erase the fact that it's not baptism as designed and decreed by the Holy Spirit. However, there are millions—if not tens of millions, or even hundreds of millions—of people alive on this planet today who believe they have been "baptized" because they were sprinkled or because a priest put a drop of water on their head as a baby. These well-meaning people have not been baptized according to the Bible.

When we all stand before God someday, by whose definition do you think He will determine whether or not a person was baptized? Do you suppose He will rule by the definition He gave when He inspired the Scripture? Or do you think He will defer to the definition of men who, by willful intent or ignorance, decided for their own theological reasons to change the meaning of the word?

When I teach anywhere in the world, I explain terminology/definition change as follows: I can call the microphone that I am using to amplify my voice a Ping-Pong table. I can then go overseas where people have never seen a microphone or a Ping-Pong table, show the microphone to them, and say, "This is called a Ping-Pong table." I may even become so effective in my persuasion that over time, everybody in that country will believe that a microphone is, in fact, called a Ping-Pong table. Someday, maybe even the whole world will call it a Ping-Pong table, but the reality is that no matter what I call it, it is still not a Ping-Pong table; it's a microphone.

What do these illustrations have to do with defining the terms of *missions* and *missionaries*? A mission was simply the act of taking the Gospel to people groups (tribal or ethnic groups) who had never before heard the Gospel. Anytime that plan is carried out, the act of missions has been performed. Anytime anything less than that or other than that is done, it is not wrong. However, that is not doing missions.

Is it wrong to feed hungry people? No. Final Frontiers feeds thousands and thousands of hungry people every week. Currently more than a quarter million meals are being provided each month. Is it a sin for our ministry to do that? No, but feeding hungry people is not missions; it is a "ministry" of the local churches in which we are involved, and the families and churches should also help finance it. Final Frontiers is performing this "ministry" because someone went there as a "missionary" and birthed a local church from which others can now "minister."

In other words, missions was the act of going to that village which, as far as anyone knew, had never had a clear Gospel presentation and establishing a local, self-propagating, Bible-believing, Bible-teaching church and equipping them to do the work of the ministry which includes caring for the widow and orphans and feeding those who are hungry, visiting those in prison, etc. How is that goal accomplished? Missionaries are sent in to preach the Gospel to people who have never before heard the message, to convert them, to baptize them, and to see to it that they are thoroughly taught God's Word. The primary purpose is to equip these villagers to do the same in the villages beyond them. In this way of doing missionary work, Village A hears the Gospel, then Village B hears it, and Village C, and so on until the entire region becomes exposed to the Word of God as well as to the message of the grace and glory of God. This missions process starts with missionaries and ends with ministers.

Does it really matter? Yes, I believe it does. Words have meanings, and meanings have consequences.

Years ago my father underwent heart by-pass surgery. In order to get to his heart, the doctors had to use a scalpel to cut through his chest; then they split his sternum and spread it apart. Ouch! Was a heart surgeon needed to cut through that outer layer of skin? Of course not. On the other hand, suppose the surgeon had asked an intern or nurse to cut through the skin (and he may well have). Does that make the intern or nurse a heart surgeon? Absolutely not! It is true that both sliced the skin; however, one member of the medical team did far more than the others because he was trained, equipped, and experienced.

By following that logic, suppose every medical position was labeled as "doctor." They do not perform any different duties. They still weigh the patients, take the patients' pulse and blood pressure, and even change the bed pans. The only difference to be noted is a difference in title. Now they are all called "doctors." What will the end result be? No one will have any idea who the real "doctor" is or worse yet, what a real doctor is. The importance and need of the "real" doctor will be diminished. Unqualified people will be wreaking havoc on patients around the world. The costs would be astronomical and unaffordable because every position now gets the salary of a doctor, rather than that of a nurse, a technician, or a candy striper. I can only imagine what the bill would be if everyone were a doctor!

So it is with being a missionary. Just because a person passes out a tract, builds an orphanage, or repairs an engine on an airplane or Range Rover does not make him a missionary, even though missionaries also perform those kinds of duties. It may qualify him as an intern or assistant, but not as a missionary.

Why does it matter? Let me phrase it like this: Why does it matter that two men or two women are not allowed to "marry" one another? After all, *marriage* is just a word, and words don't matter, do they? When two people "live together," they are not called "married"; rather, people say they are "living together." Why? *Marriage* is just a term. These distinctions are made because words have meanings, meanings have consequences, consequences change the culture and, ultimately, the world. Abusing the use of a word can change its very definition, and the very act of changing the definition today will change the culture (or doctrine) tomorrow.

Because the definition of the term *missionary* has been abused over the past few decades, the position, the character, and the qualifications of this preliminary gift of God to the church has also been abused. Real missions has been substituted by any number of well-meaning, needy, and praiseworthy ministries to the point that most missionaries serving around the world today are not even preachers. Sadly, statistically, most missionaries will not plant a new church or train another man for the ministry in their entire career. When that missionary presence leaves, no one has been trained to take his place except another foreign "missionary." The national church, which had no concept of the Biblical definition, is now by example producing "ministers" rather than "missionaries" and is totally unaware of their error.

The church of God stops expanding because the expanders

have been replaced by the maintainers. The maintainers do not go out in search of unreached villages or unreached tribes. They stay in their own churches and make a career out of preaching in the jails on Sunday or passing out tracts on the streets. They do what they saw their "missionary" doing, and the world continues to go unreached.

Add to that the fact that missions funding for real missionaries is being consumed by non-missionary missionaries rather than going to church planters. Of course, that outgo is perfectly acceptable for those who want to use their missions funding in that manner. However, the dilemma of where to use the missions monies is a great part of the cause that has created a vacuum in church planting funding. In recent years statistics reveal that only $1 out of every $100 given to churches in America is actually used to fund missionaries. Eighty percent of those dollars earmarked for missions actually go to support social causes rather than starting new churches. Of the remaining 20 cents, 19 are used to fund missionaries who are serving in lands that have some exposure to the Gospel, and only one cent is used to fund missioners who are going to preach to the World A population that has never even heard the name of Jesus.

Are you still wondering if abusing the term *missionary* matters? For the remainder of this book, please realize that whenever *missions* is addressed, I am referring to the Biblical definition as opposed to the modern, cultural, hijacked definition. Again, let me stress that I am not opposed to the work that other people do; I applaud them. Final Frontiers also performs ministry through the auspices of Christian television, radio, or writing tracts and books (like this one). Final Frontiers also performs other ministries such as establishing Bible institutes and colleges or providing grade school education or instructing mothers in hygiene in these poorer places. Likewise, our other ministries also become involved in feeding hungry children and widows (in fact we currently provide more than a quarter million meals per month around the world), or providing medical and dental care, or smuggling Bibles into Islamic and closed countries.

To those who are ministering in various ways, please continue to do so, do more, encourage others to join you, and do it to the glory of God. However, please don't call it *missions*; rather, refer to it proudly and honestly for what it is—ministry. Doing otherwise dilutes the term and weakens the definition God gave to *missions*. Those who call their ministry work *missions* deny the very gift and calling of God on their life because as I have already explained, He did not call everybody to be missionaries. A missionary is called to plant the church, but the process of maturing the believer belongs to the evangelist, the prophet (preachers and teachers), and the pastors who train the converts to do the work of the "ministry" and bring the people to spiritual maturity. After all, if everyone wants to be called the quarterback, then who will call the play in the huddle?

Professional chefs do not allow their interns to be called a "chef," nor would an intern dare to call himself one. First, he would be reprimanded by the chef, and secondly, he knows he would diminish the term itself because he is not qualified to hold the title. A surgeon does not allow his intern to be called a "surgeon," nor would the intern dare to do so for the same reasons. This point is true for welders, the police, the military, and nearly all trades. Congressional aides are proud to be what they are, and some may even know more about the job than does the newly elected congressman whom they serve. Still, they do not refer to themselves as congressmen, and they would be ashamed to work for a boss who did not call himself a congressman. Pit crews are highly skilled and motivated people who are honored to hold and have their positions, but they would never call themselves a driver. They know they cannot do what the driver does, and they are fully aware that he cannot do what the pit crew does.

I believe calling everybody a missionary who does ministry

work outside of a local church or in an area that is not where they live degrades the position and the definition of *missionaries*. After all, these so-called missionaries may have a different calling on their lives. I would not want to be called a "pastor," and I don't think pastors would want to be called a "missionary" either.

Let me share an example. When I was a boy, I wanted to learn how to witness to people. A layman in my church, East Lake Baptist Church in Atlanta, named Bobby Oswalt had a great burden for men who were in prisons. Every Sunday after lunch, he would go to various prisons or jails in the Atlanta area to witness to prisoners. One Sunday he asked if any of the boys in his Sunday school class would like to go. I wasn't in his class, but my older brother David was, and David happened to mention the invitation. I wanted to go so badly, but I wasn't yet old enough. For some reason, none of his Sunday school boys were able to go, but I wanted to go so badly that it hurt.

Every story I could remember was of an old man, like Moses or Abraham, serving God. I remember thinking to myself, "I can't wait until I am old and gray so that I can serve God too." Out of the blue seemingly came this opportunity to visit with Brother Oswalt, but alas, I was still too young. In desperation, I finally asked him, "Can I go?" I expected he would say no because I wasn't old enough to be in his class. To my surprise, he agreed to take me if it was acceptable to my father. Thankfully, I had a dad who never did anything in his life to discourage any of us from serving God, so he gave a cheerful affirmation to Mr. Oswalt. The two of us began going to the jails.

Week after week I would listen to him witness to the prisoners and watch him lead them to Christ. Finally, several months later, just he and I made the venture on one day, and there were more cells than he could visit. I really wanted to strike out and imitate what I had learned from him, but I was so shy, so nervous, and so afraid. For a few moments, like Jacob on a dusty hill, I wrestled with the Lord, and every punch of an excuse I gave, He counterpunched me, knocking me to the floor, so-to-speak. I rocked back and forth, wanting to move but being afraid to, until finally I walked away from Brother Oswalt toward the noise I could hear coming from a cell that had seven men in it in the far back of the building.

Scared to death as a 12-year-old boy, I led my first souls to Christ that day. Five of the seven men accepted our Lord. One of them with tears rejected Christ, refusing to accept Him, though knowing that he should. One of them slept through the entire presentation of the Gospel. (It is still common for people to sleep through my sermons 43 years later!) Bobby kept this schedule every Sunday for years—for as long as I knew him. I haven't seen Bobby Oswalt in probably 40 years, and as far as I know, if he's still alive, he's still visiting the prisons, winning souls to Christ. Bobby never one time that I know of went to a church and asked people to support him in his prison ministry. He never one time, as far as I knew, referred to himself as a missionary to the prisons. You see, the term *missionary* had not yet changed its meaning in 1968. The idea of a missionary's being a church planter would not begin to disintegrate for another ten or fifteen years.

Today, throughout America, hundreds of men work to raise support as missionaries to the prisons. The idea behind seeking support is, "You should support me so that I can quit my secular job and be full-time in the ministry of preaching in jails." Those who support him assume that he is doing that every day (and I am sure that some do). Is it wrong to support these people as missionaries to the prisons? I believe it is. I do not believe it is wrong to support them; I believe it is wrong to support them as missionaries. Why? Because they are not missionaries; they are evangelists. They are not going to a place and probably not even to a people and certainly not to a people group who have never been exposed to the name of Jesus Christ and to the Gospel of our Saviour. That is what a missionary does.

So why do they call themselves "missionaries?" For one of

two reasons: the first being ignorance and the second being the reality that they think no church will support them as an "evangelist," but they will be easily supported as a "missionary." To them I would say, "Remember the example of Lester Roloff."

Speaking to those unspoken to is what Paul and Timothy did, among others who are examples of missionaries in the New Testament. You might say, "Well, what about James?" What about him? He was not a missionary; he was the pastor of the church at Jerusalem, and Jerusalem was no longer a mission field.

As K.P. Yohannan accurately stated in his book, *Revolution in World Missions*, Jerusalem ceased to be a mission field after Pentecost and became a parish. The people were having church every day, from house to house. The people there knew the Word of God because the Jews had been taught it in their schools since childhood; everybody in Jerusalem knew Who Jesus was, including the Romans as well as the visitors from the known world. Everyone who lived there knew what had just happened weeks before Pentecost. They knew how Jesus had been crucified and raised from the dead. Jerusalem was not a mission field. Claiming to be a missionary to Jerusalem in the days after Pentecost would be comparable to walking into the First Baptist Church of Atlanta and witnessing to the members, thinking that you are a missionary. No, you are not! You are a preacher or maybe an evangelist or an exhorter. You are whatever you are, but you are not a missionary—even if you came from Korea or Kenya to speak to these church people. Where you are from compared to where you are serving is not what makes you a missionary.

My point is this: when the title of missionary is used so freely by every person who does any ministry outside of a local church, what a missionary really is and does has been diminished.

❖

I have already mentioned my friend Tommy Tillman, who is a missionary to the lepers in Southeast Asia. He, along with

Bobby Oswalt, had the greatest influence on my life in the ministry. Bobby was used in my life when I was a young boy, and God used Tommy in my life when I was a teenager.

With the fun-loving personality he has, Tommy decided to write a gag letter to his supporting churches. You know how jokesters are. He used some crazy, typically Southern name that only Tommy could come up with. The impetus of his letter went something like this: "My name is Bubba Bodunkas. I live in Southern Louisiana, and I have been walking on the beach. I am disturbed by the sight of dead seagulls being washed up on the shore. They have all been shot with birdshot, and I spotted a fellow walking on the beach with a shotgun, shooting at the seagulls flying overhead. I am so concerned about the destruction of the seagulls, that I have decided to become a missionary to the seagull killers. That is my purpose for sending this letter to your church. I want you to consider supporting me in this endeavor."

Keep in mind, this was a gag letter that Tommy sent out from his own office on some fabricated letterhead that said, "Bubba Bodunkas, Missionary to the Seagull Killers, New Orleans, Louisiana." Obviously, anyone who was really observant would have realized the return address was his. Would you believe that he received three checks in the mail from three of his supporting churches? Three different churches sent support to a "missionary to seagull killers," sight unseen!

Every kind of "missionary" seeks support. It's time for America's churches to get back to what supporting missions really is and not what their ignorance or ego would like it to be.

It was October 18, 1992, when I found myself in the city of Londonderry, New Hampshire. George Bush had just been defeated by Bill Clinton who had been sworn into office. I had been invited to be the speaker at the mission's conference being held at the Londonderry Bible Church. I was not alone as there were some seven or eight other missionaries present with their families. This was in the early years of our ministry. The term *national preacher* was finally beginning to be accepted in our church verbiage as an actual term with meaning. Still, most had not yet comprehended that all pastors are national pastors. As I would hear the other missionaries present talking about me under their breath and mocking me, I couldn't help but grieve over the fact that as they berated the *nationals*, they were also unwittingly berating themselves.

There was at the conference a young couple, Mark and Laura Glodfelter, who eagerly seemed to listen to all I had to say and were intrigued by our method of doing missions. Before the week was over, I approached them about going to work for Final Frontiers. I was delighted to have acquired new "converts," but their eagerness was soon dissolved when their home pastor told them to avoid Final Frontiers because he had never heard of us. Obediently they went on to England as missionaries—lasting less than a term and returning home disillusioned by the unethical practices of the missionary they had been sent to assist. That particular missionary, now divorced and out of the ministry, was spending his time and consuming his support, not in preaching and planting churches, but in traveling around Europe and buying ancient Biblical manuscripts which he then sold for a hefty profit. Mark returned home discouraged but correctly saying that he didn't go to England to sell Bibles, and if that was what he was going to have to do, he might as well return home.

Mark's pastor has probably still never heard of Final Frontiers except for that one event when Mark introduced us to him. No matter though, in spite of being unknown, we are now operating in more countries than most any other Baptist missions organization and have more on-the-ground missionaries than any other Baptist organization except for the Southern Baptist Convention. And I boldly make a distinction between having missionaries who are on furlough or deputation as opposed to those who are serving on the field at any given moment. You see, most mission agencies will have at least 20 percent of their missionaries on furlough at any given time and at least that many or more "missionaries" who are just starting or still on deputation (and may never even make it to the field). In addition, many agencies count husband and wife as two. We don't. We could, we just don't. Now where was I? Oh yes...

That week during the evening services, each night a different missionary was assigned to teach a combined children's class while I spoke each night to the youth and adults in the auditorium. The "fellowship hall" was decorated by the missionary displays on tables that were lining the circumference of the hall. Each night after the service, we would all stand dutifully by our displays, hoping to speak to the members who gathered for coffee and snacks. It was on one of those evenings as most of the church members had left that Mark and his wife came over to see me and commented on how the other missionaries were mocking my "display."

You see, I don't have one. All I do, as many already know, is to place portfolios of various preachers in need of support on my table and copies of our *Progress Report*. I guess I could make a display, but I am there for a purpose, and that purpose is not to entertain with trinkets, foreign "canned goods," and photos of tourist traps. My job is to get preachers sponsored—nothing more, nothing less, nothing else.

On the last night of the conference, the pastor had all the church assemble in the auditorium and asked the children to show the pictures they had drawn based on the stories that the missionaries had taught them. For some reason he had selected the third or fourth grade boys class to write a summary of "What Missionaries Do." Remember now, this was to be done in their own words based on the lessons they had been taught and testimonies they had heard each night in their combined children's classes.

As the program continued, we all admired the pictures and enjoyed the missionary songs they had learned. Then a little boy stepped to the microphone, and he proudly announced that during the week they had learned all about what missionaries do. He then summarized all he had heard into a list of three things. I am sure his parents and all the others were waiting with anticipation to hear what their children had learned and could not but wonder how this knowledge would or could affect the rest of their lives. Pausing to take a breath, the young boy said, "The three things that missionaries do is...number one, they kill snakes; number two, they work in the garden; and number three, they don't get enough people to come to church."

The congregation was stunned, and for a brief moment that seemed like an eternity, a pharaoh's tomb had more sound and movement than that church did. I was shocked to think what those children had gleaned from all the missionary testimonies, and at the same time, I was embarrassed for the missionaries. And then, I was angry—not at the children, not even at the missionaries—but at the reality that this is the stuff that failure is made from.

No wonder our youth are not volunteering for missions if this is the image we present to them. It is an image of sloth, laziness, and incompetence. Not that those descriptions were deserved, but by what they had taught for five nights, that is what the children came away with. Deserved or not, that was the image they gave of a missionary's life and ministry.

When I was growing up, missionaries were presented to me as the heroes of the faith. In my eyes, they were giants—like spiritual Paul Bunyans chopping away at the gates of Hell. They were the masters of their lands, the overseers of God's vineyards, the ambassadors of Heaven. They could, as King David, run through a troop or leap over a wall. They were God's "mighty men."

When they spoke at our church, I would try to sit next to them or behind them. My family would take them out to eat or host them in our home, and I would sit up for hours at night listening to them tell their stories of spiritual conquest. I never expected a missionary could even spell the word *failure*—much less be one.

We were blessed that week to get a number of preachers sponsored. Some of those same families still support their national preachers faithfully every month though many have moved to other churches in other states. What abundant fruit they have stored up in their Heavenly accounts after these many years! Mark now pastors the Walnut Avenue Baptist Church in Pensacola, Florida, and has led their church to support a number of preachers and children through our ministry. I always tease him that some day he will get right with God and come back to missions. Our doors are open to him when that day comes.

Did you know that 91 percent of all Christian outreach does not target non-Christians but rather other Christians in World C countries?

Did you know that the majority of the unreached people groups are in countries that have restricted access? Western missionaries may not even be able to get to them.

CHAPTER 3

What Is a Mission Field?

Did you know that approximately 80 percent of all monies given to missions by North American believers is used specifically for the funding of social causes—not for the direct preaching of the Gospel?

Where Can a Mission Field Be Found?

N ow that I have addressed what a missionary really is (or should be), allow me to look with more detail at what a mission field is. Perhaps the three segments to this unit—"what is missions," "what is a missionary," and "what is a mission field" could have been addressed as one topic, but please, bear with me again as I touch on what a mission field is and where one can be found.

As I have already stated, Jerusalem ceased to be a mission field after Pentecost and would have been better classified as a parish. There was no recorded effort of the early churches' sending "missionaries" to Jerusalem. Many of them (referred to as apostles) resided in the city, so one may argue that Jerusalem was a field.

Personally, I would disagree. Apostles in Jerusalem were living there and in the surrounding towns before the Commission was given. Jerusalem was what I call home base. What was occurring in Jerusalem for at least a short time was saturation evangelism, as Acts 5:42 declares. *"And daily in the temple, and in every house, they ceased not to teach and preach Jesus Christ."* Jerusalem, that is, the church located within the city became the center of Christianity for a time and was the seat of its dogma and leadership worldwide.

After 70 A.D. when Christ's prophesies of Jerusalem's destruction in Matthew 24 were completed, that city "center," or what was left of it, was moved to Antioch. The "churches" solidified their individual autonomy and grew naturally without a central organization or any international leading body. They continued to expand by sending out missionaries to regions that had not yet been exposed to the Gospel.

However, some of its remnants later perverted original doctrine and practices by merging with and introducing pagan idolatry, dogma, and ritual. These remnants became known as the Roman Church with its offshoots in Syria, Egypt, Armenia, Russia, etc.

Up to that time, Jerusalem and the Jews were in some ways like Western nations today, as far as evangelism is concerned. They were locked into a philosophy and methods that could only be broken with the rod of the Diaspora. They would not, or perhaps could not, adapt to new methods and philosophies of reaching the Gentiles rather than targeting only the Jews until the Lord forced it on them. God used a zealous Peter with a repeating dream to initiate this evangelism. After all, it took the influence and charisma of a Peter to "pull it off"; but even he was initially chided for his breach of etiquette when he dared enter the home of and witness to a Gentile—and a Roman officer at that.

Whereas Peter "stuck his toe in the waters of Gentile evangelism," Paul jumped head first into the deep end. He too suffered the rumors, accusations, and cursing of the "elders" both in the faith and out of the faith, but because he stayed true to his calling, I am writing these words today, and you are reading them. Otherwise, we might still be worshipping Thor and his cohorts as our fathers did until Paul or one of his disciples converted them.

How has their example been followed? Soul-winning Christians have made it a practice for decades to initiate their evangelistic efforts with the question, "If you were to die today, do you know for sure that you would go to Heaven?" Because this culture is so rooted in Scripture, that is not a confusing question to ask. However, missionaries then as now must find a way to initiate their witnessing that is culturally understandable and acceptable. The Jews had a thorough background in the Old Testament and its Messianic prophesies and understood that many of their own race had already accepted Jesus as the promised Messiah, before and certainly after Pentecost. Even Aristobulus (also called Eubulus) the younger brother of Herod Agrippa, (and also Peter's father-in-law) had not only accepted Him but was also among the 70 who were sent out by Jesus and were serving as missionaries at that time (Romans 16:10; II Timothy 4:21). The Jews then would have to choose to accept or reject that assertion, and thus witnessing for them was the act of proving from the Old Testament that Jesus was in fact the Messiah. They knew the ramifications of rejecting Him, if in fact He was *Emmanuel*, "God with us." They were rejecting God Himself—just as their forefathers had done repeatedly.

But the missionaries could not begin their witness to a Gentile in the same way. To the Greeks, death was final; there was no concept of resurrection. In fact, according to Acts 17, the mere mention of the resurrection was a source of mocking and rejection of the entire Gospel itself. For Paul to ask the "if-you-were-to-die-today" question would have been senseless to them. Death was in the hands of the gods, and no man could speculate on when his day would come unless he had been to the Oracle in Delphi or unless like Socrates, he was awaiting an appointed day of execution. Heaven was, by their understanding, completely unknown to them, so there was no desire to go there and no fear of loss in not going there. Hell, or Hades as they called it, and as it is often referred to in the New Testament, was merely the place or the abode of the dead. Hades was not a joyous place, but it was certainly not a place of fire and brimstone.

By the same token, in a soul winner's zeal to witness for Christ today, he does not comprehend that this method may be no longer culturally acceptable or even wise in some cultures. In this age of terrorism and senseless crime, imagine approaching a stranger today, looking that man in the eye, and asking him the "if-you-were-to-die-today" question. Now compound the effect by imagining that the one doing the asking is an olive-skinned, black-haired, "Arab"-looking Christian trying to witness at "Ground Zero" in New York City on any upcoming September 11. If the man being approached has never before heard the question, he may mistake the soul winner for some kind of wacky serial killer or suicide bomber!

I realize that many still use this method of witnessing and have good results, but I have been in many a place where to ask such a question would imply that you were about to kill the person to whom you were speaking. Most of those places were outside of the civil confines of the United States, but some were in the ghettos of America's major cities. Witnessing simply must be adapted to the culture. After all, salvation results from the message—not the method of delivering it.

❖

So, what is a mission field?—Well, if missions is the act of taking the Gospel to those who have never before heard the message of salvation, then a mission field would be that place where such people live. New York City is not a mission field. I know that statement will disappoint and even anger some people—especially those who like to take their youth groups on a summer "missions trip" to New York City. Please let me explain.

I graduated from Bible college in 1977 and moved to the New York City area with a group of people to start a church.

Some of those who made this move have already gone to be with the Lord. (The leader and pastor of our group was Max Helton, who later founded Motor Racing Outreach. With us was his family, the Bob Ross family, Melba Largent, Barb Czuhajewski, and several other ladies.) We went out on our own with no support and no deputation. While we were there, I met others who had come to New York City around the same time, and one was a young man I had personally grown up with from my home church, Forest Hills Baptist Church, pastored by Curtis Hutson.

I took a job teaching at a Christian school across the Hudson River in Saddlebrook, New Jersey, in order to buy groceries. My father and mother gave me a gasoline credit card so I could have gas for my car. Until sometime later, it never occurred to me that I should ask people to support me.

When I began to meet with some of my friends who were also in that area, I learned that they had gone on deputation to raise support as missionaries to New York City before moving there. I found that concept to be somewhat strange, but I noticed it did allow them to be full-time in the ministry. After a semester or so of teaching, I thought to myself, "I didn't come here to teach school; I came here to start a church. I'm having to spend so many hours teaching and driving back and forth to the school that I'm not getting anything done." So I decided then that I would quit teaching and live by faith. I wrote a few letters, sent them out, and raised enough support to live on. I received about $500 a month in support, and in 1978, I could survive though my rent alone consumed nearly a third of that support money.

These friends of mine, who were all good guys, were receiving support in 1977 and 1978 as "missionaries to New York City." Some of them are still being supported as missionaries to New York City in 2011. To me, this scenario is a bit ridiculous. They are witnessing to people, leading them to Christ, getting them baptized, and teaching them the Word of God. A part of the Great Commission—teaching—includes teaching the members about tithing and giving offerings to support the work of the ministry and to support the pastor. Their own churches should have been paying their salary as pastor— not churches across America.

So, why do churches in Omaha and Dallas and San Diego and Augusta and Minneapolis need to continue supporting these so-called missionaries to New York City? After all, are churches all across America giving your pastor his salary, or is your church giving your pastor his salary? The answer is simple: churches continue to support them because generally, once someone is added to a church's support list, he stays there until he dies or until another pastor comes on the scene with a different agenda. No church likes to drop a missionary because of the guilt feelings that result when they do so. However, if the missionary gives his supporting churches an excuse to do so by not writing, by changing doctrine, or God forbid, by moving to a new "field," then most churches will leap at the opportunity to purge him from their support list and save the ever dwindling missions funds.

So what is a mission field? A mission field is an area where there are people (and literally a culture or subculture) who have not been exposed to the Gospel. The argument is not that many people in New York City have not heard the Gospel. I have personally met people in jails who have not heard the Gospel, and I have met people who live a block away from a Baptist church who have never heard the Gospel. That is not what I'm saying. It's not that these people have not personally heard the Gospel message, but that there has not been exposure to that message. A missionary is someone who goes and brings the Gospel to those who have never before been exposed to it.

Take for example, the man from Macedonia who appeared to Paul in a dream in Acts 16:9 saying, *"Come over into Macedonia, and help us."* He did not know anything about the

Gospel. The centurion who sent servants to find Peter and bring him back to preach to his household had only gotten a glimpse of the Gospel, and he wanted to be exposed to it. As a result, he and his entire household were converted. The Philippian jailer did not know anything about the Gospel except what he heard Paul and Silas singing in the prison. When he realized what was going on, he asked in Acts 16:30, *"Sirs, what must I do to be saved?"* And he took them to his own home, and his entire family converted. Multitudes and multitudes of examples exist of true mission fields.

In fact, all the countries of the world where missionaries are sent may not necessarily be mission fields as countries go, but they may be or contain some regionally or as individual tribes or clans. For example, years ago a missionary to China named Hudson Taylor started the China Inland Mission. As a missionary in these early days of the "Modern-Day Missions Movement," he recognized the fact that most missionaries stayed safely along the coast of China in Hong Kong and in Shanghai, maybe venturing as far inland as Guangzhou (now known as Canton). The knowledge that they were not going deeper into China branded a burden into his heart to reach the masses who lived in China's interior. So he started the China Inland Mission and became famous for what he was able to do in evangelizing China. As a result, others imitated him by following suit and starting the African Inland Mission, the Sudan Interior Mission, and on and on the list goes.

Why? Had China never heard the Gospel? Yes, the people living all along the coast had exposure to the Gospel, but all the villages inland had not. Did Hudson Taylor not have a burden for those living on the coast? Of course he did. Had every person in every hamlet, village, town, and city along the coast received a personal "if-you-were-to-die-today" witness? Of course not. So then why did Taylor abandon the masses along the coast in the biggest cities and in the largest and most densely populated region of China to go inland to the native

Chinese, the tribal peoples, the uneducated, and the illiterate masses? Hudson Taylor understood that these people also needed the Gospel, and no one else was willing to take the message to them. His burden revived a doctrine that had been misunderstood and incorrectly taught in the seminaries of Christendom, the realization that the Commission is directed toward evangelism and church planting among every nation, literally defined as "ethnic groups," and not to fluctuating geographical boundaries.

Incidentally, in an effort to become like the Chinese so he could better reach them, Taylor abandoned his European style of clothing and wore the clothes of the "coolie," an ordinary laborer. He wore the traditional skull cap, grew out his hair and wore it in the "queue" (pigtail), a coolie's traditional hairstyle. He also left the relative safety of the missionary compound and lived with a Chinaman in a boarding house so that he could give his full attention to learning and "becoming" Chinese. As a result, his mission board fired him, and all the good churches dropped his support. Still he persevered and made history.

Now here's a question for you: most Christians know the name of Hudson Taylor, but can you name just one of the "spiritual" veteran missionaries on the board who fired him— I didn't think so.

I have a particular fondness for the nation of Honduras, which most certainly has been exposed to the Gospel. I know of seven Christian television stations in Honduras, or at least in the capital city. Probably everyone there has access to the Gospel. Whether or not they have actually heard the Gospel message is a different issue. Outside of the city and after traveling by burro or footpath, people can be found who have not been exposed to the Gospel. Generally, they know the name of Jesus because of the Catholic upbringing for the last 500 years in the country of Honduras. However, they do not know the first thing about Who Christ really is or what He has done for them and what He wants to do for them. They have no idea how He sacrificed His life for them so they could escape eternal damnation and live with Him and His Father in Heaven forever. They don't know these truths, so this is clearly a mission field existing within a "country" that may no longer really qualify as a mission field. Typically, as long as there are pockets of people groups or regions that had no exposure, that country is still referred to as a mission field. Perhaps the "country" itself should not be classified as a mission field; that decision is up to the individual. On the other hand, you should be informed that there are still five barely-reached or unreached ethnic groups living in Honduras. These people are definitely a mission field.

In Guatemala dozens of villages of ethnic groups (tribes) of Mayan descent have had no exposure to the Gospel. They still wear their tribal costumes, eat the food of their ancestors prepared in the same manner, and speak the language of their fathers. In fact, many of these people do not speak Spanish; thus, they have had no exposure to Christ.

What must be done in order to fulfill the Great Commission is to begin to see the world as a collection of ethnic groups—not nations. My first ministry was to the Akha people in Thailand, but the Akha also live in Myanmar, Laos, Vietnam, and China. Each is a sub-group of the unit. Their culture is basically the same as are their traditions because they are not separated by geographical boundaries though those boundaries are clearly visible on a map. The Akha are a nation, just like the Cherokee, the Apache, and others Native Americans were referred to as "nations." Did the Jews cease to be a nation when they were taken into captivity by Nebuchadnezzar? No! They adopted the Babylonian, then Mede, then Persian lifestyle, clothing, language, and culture, but they remained Jews to such an extent that Cyrus could easily replant them in their own homeland 70 years later.

Perhaps the sheep should be separated from the goats in

this point by describing Biblically what is not a mission field. It's not the county fair. It's not the hometown jail. It's not the courtroom or the courthouse. These are places where believers should go and evangelize and exert an influence, but they are not mission fields. They are places of need and ministry opportunities, but once a culture has been exposed to the Gospel and has begun to ingest it, that culture is no longer a "mission" field. It is a field of service. Rather, it is a place in need of the evangelist, the preacher, the pastor, and the teacher. The good work has already begun; the foundation has already been laid. Now it is time to erect the structure.

I once read that some 85 percent of the missionaries serving today are working in 13 countries. That statistic, if true, is incredible. It supports the point I am trying to make as to what a mission field is. That statistic means there are still 181 countries of the world (194 minus the 13), and all the ethnic groups living within these countries, who still have no exposure to the Gospel. This knowledge of the unreached ethnos is what has spurred missions from the time of Paul. Hudson Taylor saw the coastal Chinese as having the Gospel laid out before them over and over, while those in the interior went without exposure. Not a single missionary was willing to venture into the inland regions to reach the Chinese whom missionaries purportedly had such a burden to reach. Was it possible that their sponsors only intended for them to reach those at the mouth of the Yellow River but not those at its headwaters? Though Taylor ignited a missionary fire that still burns, the problem remains; the same stale concept of missions that he had to fight still crops up today.

When pastors speak to me regarding a missions strategy for their church, one of the things I recommend the most is to target the ethnic groups—not the countries. Otherwise, those most in need—who are waiting for some future Samaritan to deem their cause worthy enough to interrupt his schedule, dire enough to expend his fortune, and pitiful enough to leave the smooth road on which he is traveling to go to them where they are and as they are—will continue to be passed by—ignored and unreached.

Most Christians today do not know the true definition of a missionary. They believe as I always did, until I became involved in missions work, that a missionary is simply someone who goes from "here" to "there" to preach or someone who leaves his country to go to another country to start and pastor a church. Of course, there are exceptions with those who stay in their own country but go to other regions or states to be missionaries. That is why preachers from Georgia go to Wyoming, and preachers from Wyoming go to Alaska, and preachers from Alaska go to Maine. They are called "missionaries," whereas the other preachers ministering in those same states are called "pastors." The only real difference is that the pastors are being funded by their own congregation or secular work, and the missionaries are being funded by churches across America. I have actually been in churches where the members did not know that their pastor referred to himself as a "missionary" and had income from churches across America.

About a year ago a young man and his wife came to the church I attend in Augusta, Georgia, and asked our church to support them as missionaries to a suburb of Atlanta. There are over 5,000 Baptist churches in Atlanta, not to mention other Bible-believing churches. One can practically stand on the front porch of any church and throw a stone to the next church, crisscrossing the entire metropolis.

This young man said he was called to be a missionary to Atlanta. I would question the need for Atlanta to have another church, but if God has called that young man to be a missionary to Atlanta, he certainly needs to do what God has called him to do. But to call himself a missionary to Atlanta doesn't just border on the absurd; it jumps into the deep waters of totally misunderstanding the definition of what a missionary really is!

If I move from Augusta to Atlanta to start a church, am I a missionary? What if I move from the suburb of Decatur to the suburb of Stone Mountain, just ten miles away? Does that move make me a missionary? If I move from the south side of Fulton County where the airport is to the north side or downtown area and live in a high-rise apartment, does that make me a missionary? What if I just walk across the street and give a man a tract? Does handing out a tract make me a missionary? The answer to all of these questions is a resounding "no," yet pastors often tell their people that when they witness or pass out a tract, they are a missionary. Really? By that same logic if I screw in a new light bulb, it makes me an electrician. When I carve the Thanksgiving turkey, it makes me a butcher. And when I give my wife a spoonful of cough syrup, I instantly become a doctor.

What then is a missionary? A missionary is someone who takes the Gospel to someone who has never before heard the Gospel message. A missionary is not someone with blond hair and blue eyes going to preach to someone with black hair and brown eyes. That is not missions. I know people who left America 30 years ago to start a church on a mission field, and they still serve in that same church. May I say, in my humble and often incorrect opinion, they are not missionaries. They are pastors in a foreign country because a missionary is not a permanent pastor. A missionary is a church planter who pastors for a limited time and then turns that church work over to someone else who's called to pastor; then he does what he's called to do—be a missionary. In other words, he leaves the church, walks down the village path or gets in his vehicle, or whatever the case may be, and goes to the next village he can find that has never had an exposure to the Gospel. He then plants himself there for a day, a week, a month, a year, or maybe six years as some say Paul did in Corinth. When that church is established and he has developed men who are qualified to pastor that flock, he turns it over to them, and he moves on to start the process all over again. That process is the Biblical work of a missionary.

Some bring up the point that the words *missionary* and missions are not even in the Bible. True, they are not. That fact brings me to three questions:

- What are we doing?
- Why are we doing it?
- What are we even talking about?

As a matter of fact, *missions*, as a term, is in the Bible, but as a different name. That does not mean the name is being changed; a microphone is not being called a Ping-Pong table. But when the Bible was translated, it was both translated and transliterated, depending on the availability of the word. *Translation* means "converting a word in one language to another language." *Transliteration* occurs when the word to be converted to a different language does not exist in that target language. In that case, the original word is tweaked to accommodate the culture of the other language. For example, the English word for *water* is translated *agua* in Spanish. The English word *nation* is transliterated to *nacion* in Spanish. They are the same word with the same meaning with a slightly different spelling or pronunciation due to a simple, minute cultural/grammatical difference. In fact, nearly every English word that ends with "tion," ends with a "cion" in Spanish. Congratulations! You just learned a hundred Spanish words in the time it took you to read this paragraph!

The book of Ephesians lists the gifts that have been given to the body of Christ as well as to local congregations individually. These God-given gifts help people to mature in the faith, to grow, to evangelize, and to reproduce: in essence, the directives of the Great Commission. Four positions are listed: apostles, prophets, evangelists, and pastors, but some would add a fifth, teachers. Today many lump the pastor and teacher together, believing that teaching is the role of pastor, rather than being a separate position. People generally know and understand the roles of pastor and teacher, but I often find that few people understand the roles of the apostle, the prophet, and the evangelist.

The Greek word *apostle* was later translated as "missionary." In other words, the English word *missionary* comes from the Greek word *apostle*. This translation really confuses many Christians, especially Baptists, because some Baptists do not believe that apostles exist today. Baptists believe that the apostles held a temporary position in the early church only, and that for a man to be an apostle, certain qualifications had to be met. Those qualifications primarily are taken from the book of Acts when the disciples under the leadership of Peter were looking to appoint someone as an apostle to take the place of Judas after he had betrayed Christ and had committed suicide. In that particular dissertation, Peter gave the qualifications for what an apostle should be in his opinion. (1) The man had to have been personally taught by the Saviour and (2) The man had to be a witness of the resurrection of Jesus Christ. However, many modern-day theologians also believe an apostle had to have a part in writing the New Testament as well.

Let me share why I believe these qualifications are erroneous. First, these qualifications were dictated by Peter. They were defined by Peter, and nowhere does the Bible say that God gave Peter these qualifications, that God condoned them, or that God agreed with Peter's standards. In fact, the very man who was chosen based upon Peter's distinctives was later seemingly overturned by God when He personally called and appointed Paul as an apostle to the Gentiles.

When choosing between two men by casting a long straw and a short straw, a person automatically assumes that whoever gets the designated straw is the winner. Just because these are the only two options, one of them will be chosen, but that doesn't necessarily mean that God had actually chosen the winner. All that scenario means is that there were two men and two straws and one was bound to be chosen—right or wrong.

Indeed, the resurrected Christ did appear to Paul, Jesus did teach him personally in the wilderness for a period of time, and Paul did write a portion of the Scripture.

My second disagreement is that nowhere in the Bible does it say that only apostles wrote Scripture. There were no apostles before the New Testament era, and even during the New Testament era, some of the men who wrote portions of the Scripture were not apostles. Luke, for example, was not an apostle, and as far as anyone knows, he has never been named as one. Still, he wrote the books of Luke and Acts.

Yet another point to consider is that some men who were apostles did not write any of the Bible. For example, Barnabas, who was referred to as an apostle, didn't write any Scripture; and as far as anyone knows, he was never taught by Christ and never even met Christ.

The point I am trying to make is that quite possibly we don't really understand what an apostle is. If so, it's time to stop calling a microphone a Ping-Pong table and see what God has to say in the New Testament about the example of the apostle or the missionary.

Who was the missionary? It was not Peter, and neither was it James. The example missionary to whom we look in the New Testament was Paul, who happened to be, by God's choosing, an apostle.

So what exactly is a missionary tasked to do? What is his assignment? What is his job classification? A missionary Biblically is someone who takes the Gospel to people who have never before heard it, wins the people to Christ, baptizes them, organizes them into a local church, disciples them, trains men among them to do the same, and then moves on and starts all over again, taking some of those men with him to help him in that process. That is what a missionary is designed by God to do.

The next gift that was given to the church was the prophet. Generally, the word *prophet* conjures the image of someone who foretells the future, but that definition does not exactly describe the role of a prophet. In some cases, some prophets did foretell the future. When the prophet Nathan confronted David about his sin with the wife of Uriah the Hittite and his subsequent plan for murdering Nathan, he was not foretelling the future. Rather, Nathan was exposing the hidden past and proclaiming a fact of coming judgment. He was direct and to the point, and he was saying, "David, you have sinned before God! You have committed adultery with a married woman, and you have had her husband killed to cover it up! God is going to punish you for that sin."

Even in the New Testament time, prophets were not necessarily those who were telling the future. Generally, they were those who were bluntly and boldly declaring the Word of God, and again, particularly to those people who had some understanding of Who God was and what He required. These prophets had been exposed to the Gospel, they had learned about Christ, and perhaps they even had a background in Jewish history and knew more about it than most. But these prophets did not have the complete Word of God; in fact, they may not have even had the Old Testament in their language. So the prophet follows behind the apostle, who is the planter of the church and begins to declare the Word of God to those people, helping them to grow in their faith. He does not predict God's word; he declares it and explains it more thoroughly to those who have ears to hear.

The evangelist is another Ping-Pong table, if ever there was one. Today in America, many men use the term *evangelist* to denote their position as a traveling preacher.

When I was first exposed to missions work in Asia, on my very first night of talking with some national preachers who had no exposure to America whatsoever, they asked me what I did. At that time I told them I was a pastor. I then asked each of the five men, "What are you?" Each one of the men responded that he was an evangelist. Through the interpreter I responded by commenting, "Oh, I thought you were all pastors."

To this statement they responded, "We are pastors." The men testified that they all pastored multiple churches. The one with the fewest was pastoring five; another man was pastoring seven. It confused me that they would be pastoring so many churches and yet call themselves evangelists.

So, being inquisitive, I asked, "If you are a pastor, why do you call yourself an evangelist?"

Their response, "Because we evangelize," startled me. I must have really looked confused because one of them said to me, "What do evangelists do in your country?" I thought for a moment, and with all clarity and sincerity and no intention of sarcasm, I answered, "Typically, in my country an evangelist is a man who used to be a pastor. He is retired from being a pastor and now goes to preach in churches pastored by his friends. That's what we call an evangelist."

They huddled together in the corner of the little bamboo hut, talked among themselves for a moment, and then one of them turned around to look at me, and asked, "If a man is an evangelist, why would he be preaching in churches since the people in church have already been evangelized?"

It was as if a meteorite had hit me in the head. His question changed my life forever and caused me to begin questioning everything I had ever been taught about the ministry. His question, seemingly so simple, was so profound.

His was a valid point. Why would an evangelist preach in a local church when the unsaved are outside the local church? Am I saying, "It is wrong to be an American-style evangelist? No! Am I trying to belittle men who do that? No! Am I trying to make them feel guilty or look silly to those who read this book? No! My purpose is to make a point, specifically that the definition of terms are constantly changed, and when they are, the office and importance of the original definition becomes diluted to the point that it eventually dissolves.

Pouring pure Coca Cola syrup into a glass of soda water at the improper ratio will produce a drink that tastes horrible. However, diluting it in the correct ratio produces a wonderful tasting drink. On the other hand, continuously diluting the mixture of Coca Cola syrup and soda water will eventually produce a drink that has no resemblance to a Coke. Does it still have Coca Cola in it? Yes. Does it still owe its base or its root to Coca Cola? Yes. But is it a Coca Cola? No. It is a Coca Cola that has been diluted to the point of nonrecognition. That is exactly what has been done with missions. Everything and everybody related to missions, the missionary, and the mission field, have been so tainted they do not even know what they are or were Biblically intended to be.

This brings me back to the point of this subject. How can one be a missionary if he does not know what the term means? Truthfully, I suppose the answer to that question is that he cannot be a missionary, unless it happens upon him by accident.

Some 2,000 years ago, Christ gave the Great Commission—His parting command—not a suggestion. His desire was to leave believers with the privilege and the responsibility to fulfill the Great Commission. Yet, not one generation of the church of Christ has fulfilled that command since it was given. Today I believe because of the era of technology in which we live, because of burdens and convictions, and because of the tools available to us (for lack of a better term), believers now have not only the capability of fulfilling this command, but they will also experience the reality of doing so in their lifetime. As I write this today, I am 55 years old. If I live a normal life span, I have a 100-percent conviction and belief in my heart that before I pass, the Gospel will have been given or exposed to every people group on this planet.

Photo: A tribal mud hut in central Ghana near the Volta River. This particular village has already been reached with the Gospel.

[Photo taken February 2011]

Examining
the Problems
Which Have
Caused
Failure in
Fulfilling the
Great Commission

Annual Global Christian Income in U.S. Dollars
in 2006:
$15,930,000,000,000

- Total estimated annual income given to churches and parachurch ministries: $360,000,000,000

- Given to Foreign Mission: $21,000,000,000 which is 5.8 percent of giving to all Christian causes

- Cost per baptism worldwide: $349,000

Interestingly, it is estimated that $22 billion was lost due to "ecclesiastical crimes" (embezzlement, etc.) That's more money than was spent on missions.

Introduction

Did you know it is estimated that less than one percent of all Americans who offer themselves as missionaries ever reach "the field"? Of those who do, less than half return for a second term.

The Great Commission has not been fulfilled in this lifetime primarily because of three main problems which I call the "Big Three":

- Manpower Problems
- Money Problems
- Mentality Problems

If these three issues can rightly be addressed and overcome, then the Gospel can be advanced throughout the world. Christian workers could spend the rest of their lives watching as the Gates of Hell collapse in front of them.

Number of Non-Christians
Per Missionary Serving:

Tribal/Other 17,000
Hindu 179,000
Unreligious 82,000
Muslim 306,000
Buddhist 176,000

86 percent of the world's Hindus, Muslims, and Buddhists do not personally know a Christian.

Decline of U.S. Career Missionaries:

1988 65,000
2008 35,000

In the past 20 years the number of career missionaries sent out by U.S. mission agencies has declined by over 45 percent.

CHAPTER 1

Manpower Problems

Did you know that of the 24,000 known people groups existing on the earth today, half have never had a Gospel presentation or have even heard the name of "Jesus" once?

On September 12, 2007, Avon proudly announced on their Web site that they had acquired over five million representatives worldwide. That's five million door bell ringers. How does that number compare to the number of missionaries there are worldwide?

The truth of the matter is, from a Biblical standpoint, as I have already overstated, most of the people who are called missionaries are not really missionaries. The capacity in which they serve is performing ministry work, but we refer to them as missionaries rather than ministers, and they raise support for their ministry by calling themselves missionaries.

It is a fact that most missionaries are not church planters, though there are certainly some glorious exceptions. For instance, the Baptist Bible Fellowship has traditionally required their missionaries to start a church during their first term. However, other mission boards, such as New Tribes Missions and even Campus Crusade for Christ do not allow their missionaries to start churches. As a matter of fact, some boards will fire a missionary if he plants a church. The reason for that attitude is that some boards feel they have been formed for another purpose, whether it is evangelism or teaching. For one of their missionaries to plant a church would be leaving that core calling. I have no argument with the way these boards operate. There are many parts of the body, and every member had best find out for what function he was created to fulfill and do it.

What concerns me is why churches are supporting people as missionaries who are being overseen by a board of directors who will dismiss them if they do the work of a missionary. To be fair to both of these organizations (since I have been bold enough to mention them), Campus Crusade's purpose, as I understand it, is to win the individual to Christ, disciple him and place him in a local church. Certainly there is nothing wrong with that goal. New Tribes Missions specializes in translating the Scriptures into languages that do not yet have the Bible in a printed format. Could there be a more noble cause? I think any man serving in any capacity that edifies and builds the body of Christ is worthy of support, I just think that person should be supported for what he is—not for what he isn't.

Most pastors and certainly most church members are not aware of these problems in missions today. Many people think that all missionaries are out hacking their way through a jungle with a machete in one hand, hoping to find a village of half-naked people who have never heard of Jesus and carrying a Bible in the other with which to evangelize that village. They expect that a month later the missionary will have produced a building with a steeple on it! They expect that all the native men will be dressed with white shirts and ties, and they will all be singing "Amazing Grace." That's the typical concept American churches have regarding missionaries.

The simple truth of the matter is that most missionaries will not plant a church because most missionaries are not church planters. No one argues the fact that the majority of those who are sent out as missionaries today are fulfilling other needed capacities of ministry. For instance, they may be a school teacher, an orphanage worker, an airplane mechanic, or a pilot. Most definitely these jobs are not negative, and neither are they roles that should not be done. They are all worthy and noble and needed, but they are not missions from a Biblical standpoint.

Allow me to state once again: if a person is satisfied with calling anything missions that takes somebody from point A to point B, then he is probably happy with the way missions is being handled. But if he really wants to get back to the Biblical definition and the Biblical pattern of missions, then he cannot deny the fact that current methods as well as motives have failed. The goal should be to get the Gospel to every ethnic group on the planet in this lifetime. And the next generation and the one following should have the exact same goal until as the Scripture says in Habakkuk 2:14, *"For the earth shall be filled with the knowledge of the glory of the LORD, as the waters cover the sea."* That is the ultimate goal, and until it has been reached, this generation has not succeeded as a Great Commission generation.

How will that goal be reached if the methods, the principles, and the protocols established in the Scripture are not being followed? Too many Christians seem to think that they can do it their way and that their way is better.

This arrogant attitude reminds me of the time in the Old Testament when the Jewish people were described as each man doing what was right in his own eyes. That is exactly how we do missions today. We do missions the way we think we should do it, and the churches support those whom they think they should support—with little or no understanding of the criteria that qualifies the candidate as a missionary.

The truth is, fewer missionaries are serving today than in decades past. The zeal for missions is dying, and I, for one, believe that a good reason for this slow death is because the pattern for Biblical, God-ordained responsibility of a missionary has been ignored.

When I was a young boy, I was enthralled by the stories of missionaries, what they were doing, what they had accomplished, and the struggles they had to go through. But today's stories revolve around the need to buy a new Land Rover or the need for a certain curriculum for the children's home school or the needed funding for a larger shipping container so the missionary family can take all of their belongings to the field with them. Today's requests and reports tend to go on like that. Missions work has become nothing but church work on the other side of the world or church work in another country or state.

Many missionaries don't even live in the country to which they have been "called." It is a little known fact that the majority of "missionaries to Mexico" live along the border inside the United States. What message does that give to the church members inside Mexico when their missionary/pastor resides in America? Where is his accountability? What message does that give to young boys and girls who want to be missionaries regarding how to be one, the importance of the call, and the need to forsake all, if necessary?

The truth is, the United States may no longer be the world's leader in sending out missionaries. At the most, America is barely number one followed by the tiny peninsula nation of South Korea, which leads the rest of the world in the number of missionaries being sent out. Why? The American people have become obsessed with materialism rather than servanthood. Americans, and even some American missionaries, feel that they deserve their belongings and cannot or should not live without them.

Politically, the American people tend to condemn those who feel that they are entitled, yet the same American people who decry those special privileges demand those entitlements for themselves. Spiritually or religiously, Christians act just like the world. Christians think that they are entitled to a nice house, several cars, televisions, DVD players, and video games. They are entitled to all of these amenities, and only after acquiring all these things are Christians willing to talk about giving up some of them for the Lord's service. How ridiculous!

What are Christians pursuing in their lives? Is it God's way or their way?

It's a fact that Paul didn't feel that he was entitled to do anything other than what God told him to do. In several of the epistles to various churches, Paul saw and described himself as a servant and as a slave of Jesus Christ.

So much teaching has been done in America's pulpits over the past decades about the believer's position in Christ as being an elder brother and that all believers are the beloved recipients of His redemption. Christians are told that they are special and that God loves them just the way they are. However, Christians tend not to look at their other positions in Christ.

It is true that I, Jon Nelms, am now a son of God. I have been adopted by God Almighty into His family because I have accepted the sacrifice that His Son paid on behalf of all mankind when He shed His blood on the Cross and died for their sins as a sacrifice for man.

The Bible that tells me I have the right to become the son of God because I have believed in Jesus Christ as my Saviour. True—100 percent true. I don't doubt it at all. But that does not remove the fact that I am not just His son; I am also His servant, and I am also His slave.

Modern-day Christians in the United States tend to focus on the "positive" or the "elaborate" positions that they have in Christ and tend to ignore the fact that they are also called to take up their cross and suffer. Christians are also called to lay down their lives for the Lord. They are also called to put others ahead of themselves. Believers are called to be His servants— to be His slaves.

Jesus didn't buy mankind off an auction stand. He didn't conquer them in battle and assign them as slaves to the empire. But those who have asked for His salvation have asked to be His slave. Christians feel they owe Him something; it's their reasonable service for Him. But most Americans do not understand what it means to be a slave or to be a servant.

The Christian is called to be His slave and servant, and a servant does not tell the master where he wants to go, under what conditions he will travel, or under what circumstances he will serve. A servant listens to what the master says and obeys. He doesn't question or complain. He does not ask his master's motives or motivation. He does not ask how long he will be gone, or how short a time he will be gone, what he needs to pack, or what he needs to leave behind. A servant receives an order from his master, and he obeys. That is what missionaries are supposed to be—servants of Jesus Christ.

God's command is for His servants to take the Gospel to every ethnic group on the planet—in this generation. Whether going as a servant or sending those who go, the focus, the goal, and the calling of every Christian is still the same—to see that every ethnic group on the planet receives the Gospel. However, when one observes the way churches spend money and how the leftovers go for missions, it is very obvious that church members are not being taught the importance of the Great Commission. Christians are told about missions and missionaries but assume incorrectly that they are living all over the world reaching the lost. Yet 40 percent of all foreign missionary funding is being used by missionaries in just ten "over-saturated" countries. Ten!

I don't know if this statistic is accurate or not, but I was told some 15 years ago by a missionary in the Philippines that, after World War II, over 350 Baptist missionaries were serving there. But by 1995 there were less than 30. Around 1987 I read (I don't remember what book) that by the year 2000, due to forced retirement, over 50 percent of the missionaries serving at that time (1987) would be retired and not have replacements. Thus, as the world's population was growing, the missionary force was shrinking.

Such news—true or not—further ignited the fire in me to get as many national missionaries supported as quickly as I could, and that drive has not ended to this day. At that time we were supporting preachers in two countries—Thailand, and Laos. Today we are helping God's servants in more than eighty countries.

In 1988 long after the trend toward the shrinking of the missionary force was well underway, there were still some 65,000 career missionaries serving, but by 2008 that number had shrunk to only 35,000. That's a decrease of more than 45 percent in just 20 years. It seems the "prophecy" was unfortunately true after all. And it makes me wonder what the next 20 years will hold in store.

Even though there is a manpower problem, it can be overcome simply by encouraging young people to serve God, to give a few years of their life in service for Him, to go on some mission trips, and to support missions and missionaries so that the missionaries can do what others cannot do or what others are not willing to do. Manpower is one big problem, but it is not the only problem. It is just the first one of the "Big Three."

Allocation of Mission Funding
Given by Churches:

87%   Given for missions work among those who are already Christians or fully exposed to the Gospel (World C)

12%   Given for missions work among those who have limited access to the Gospel (World B)

1%   Given for missions work among the unreached people groups

CHAPTER 2

Money Problems

Did you know that if each person in a congregation of 100 people would give one penny each day, that those pennies combined could support one national preacher full-time?

A
s I start addressing the second of the "Big Three," let me reference again the terms "World A," "World B," and "World C."

According to a report entitled *The State of World Evangelism in 2008,* from a typical $100 offering given by a church in World C (that includes America), $99.90 is spent in that local church on the membership and/or other citizen-Christians and/or local causes in one form or another. I have already addressed the fact that 80 percent of all "missionaries" stay at home! Hard to believe, isn't it? So let's examine whether or not that is a true statement.

Take a look at the "missionaries" your church is supporting and see how many of them live and work right here in the good ol' U.S.A. Does the number startle you? Fasten your seatbelt because this next statistic is really going to blow you away! From 1974-2000, nine out of ten missionaries sent out were sent to evangelize and do discipleship among those who have full access to the Gospel within their own countries, such as the United States, Australia, England, and so forth. That means they did not go anywhere. They stayed in their own land doing church work and called it missions.

In all fairness, let it be said that many of these lands are "Christian" in name only, and many who call themselves by the name of Christ have no knowledge of what it means to be born again. They do indeed need to hear the Gospel, but if they do not hear, it is because they have chosen not to listen. The Gospel is ever-present and available in those countries. These people have access to Christian churches, Christian Bible study groups, Christian coffee houses, Christian concerts, Christian Bibles, Christian tracts, Christian magazines, Christian newspapers, Christian blogs, Christian bookstores, Christian colleges, Christian schools, Christian day care, Christian television stations, Christian movies, Christian soap operas, Christian T-shirts, Christian jewelry, Christian doormats, and even the occasional witness from (you guessed it again) a Christian person. These people are without excuse.

So if $99.90 of the $100 given in a typical World C church is used in the same World C evangelized nations, where or how is that remaining ten cents used? It is earmarked for foreign missions. (Aren't you glad your church is not the typical church?)

If you think that is disgusting, just wait; I believe it gets much worse. Nine cents (out of the ten cents that is so generously given up for the sake of fulfilling Christ's Great Commission) is the amount given to evangelize the countries of the world that already have the Gospel, already have missionaries, and already have a growing, self-supporting national church. They are just not yet considered "Christian" countries. These countries comprise 39 percent of the world's population, and the combined 9 cents of all the churches fund the 17.5 percent of the world's missionary force residing in those lands. They are World B.

Are America's Christians doing enough? Absolutely not! Some countries in "World B" that are considered to be covered with the Gospel still have people groups (tribes) living within them that have little or no exposure to the Gospel. Mexico is a prime example. In 1995 the city of Puebla in Mexico already had four established Christian printing ministries turning out tracts, Gospel literature, and portions of the Bible by the hundreds of thousands. Elsewhere in Mexico are tribes that do not have a single verse of God's Word translated in their language, and many of them, especially the women, do not speak Spanish. Obviously these tribes need more missionaries, whether American or Mexican.

There is enough fruit to go around for everyone! The reality is that some of that 80 percent of the missionary force that stay at home in the comfort of America needs to go to some of these other lands and train the converts there to do what they are training the converts here to do. After all, the last time I checked, pastors, assistant pastors, evangelists, Sunday school teachers, youth workers, bus workers, soul winners, and Godly laymen are perfectly capable of doing the job the missionary is doing here in the United States.

What about the one lonely penny remaining of the $100? What is done with that one cent? That penny is what remains to spread the Gospel to the 28 percent of the world's population that has never heard the name of Jesus. Only one cent is earmarked to evangelize nearly 2 billion souls living in "World A." Only 2.5 percent of those who volunteer to be foreign missionaries go to work among these ethnic groups.

Why do I use the word *work* rather than saying "go to preach" to these people? Simply and sadly because many, if not most, "missionaries" are not preachers; they are needed, well-meaning, hard-working, dedicated, soul-winning laymen who chose to use their skills abroad in a service capacity rather than stay at home.

I take my hat off to these servants of God, and in so doing, I humbly flash my shiny bald head for all the world to see. They are champions and worthy of honor. The only problem is that the philosophy of funding these "support service" laymen and laywomen "missionaries" depletes the available resources by paying *their* salaries rather than using the same funds to support preachers and church planters. Practically speaking, most of the ten cents given to the missions funds is spent on everything the missionary needs rather than on missionaries. What a shame!

I recently viewed the Web site of a respectable ministry that works throughout the continent of Africa. Their site features a video about their various missionaries who include accountants, mechanics, teachers, nurses, dentists, and builders. Not one mention is made of an evangelist, a church planter, or a preacher. This is one of the largest and most respected mission organizations in the world, and Final Frontiers supports more of their national church planters than they do! That's because this ministry does not support ANY of them. One might legitimately wonder how much of the ten cents from each $100 that is given to missions really even goes to true Biblical missions.

Those who know me know that I am not opposed to the "social" aspect of ministry, and I am certainly not opposed to people's going to the field to work in any capacity they can. As a part of Final Frontier's overall work, programs like Touch a Life, Bags of Hope, Daily Bread, etc. feed, clothe, and educate people, build churches, build houses, dig wells, and fund Bible colleges, among various other endeavors. All of these outreach programs are done with national personnel—not with expensive exported workers from the United States. The nationals can volunteer to do the work on their own time, or if payment is necessary, they can do the work for a fraction of the cost it takes to send and support a foreigner to do that same work.

Let me attempt to illustrate the futility of the modern-day missions philosophy. If a layman or pastor or evangelist wants to put his child in a Christian school, he pays the tuition so the school can hire a teacher. The tuition payments pay the teacher's salary. But if a missionary, who earns probably as much as the average members of his supporting churches, wants to put his children in a Christian school, he enrolls them, probably without cost, and the school provides a teacher whose salary is paid by churches in America which support that teacher as a "missionary teacher." Speaking as a missionary myself, this is the question I ask: if the missionary is funded, why can't he pay for his own child's education?

The same scenario applies to the mechanic who repairs his own car or airplane, the bookkeeper who does his own accounting, the handyman who repairs the plumbing in his house, and the electrician and the builder who builds his house and church. All of these people in the work force are being paid as "missionaries" so that the missionary does not have to pay for these needs out of his support. As a result, America's churches do not have any funds left to support an actual missionary who is planting churches and witnessing day in and day out.

Call me crazy, but why can't the airplane mechanic secure a job at the airport or start his own business and repair missionary planes for free on the weekend on his own time? Why can't the handyman do the same? Isn't that what laymen do in America? Imagine if a national family in Peru, Kenya, Thailand, or any other foreign country could hire an American to come into their home and labor at "local" prices! I believe they would jump at the chance to practice their English with him and watch in great anticipation to see a white man actually work with his hands! Imagine the witnessing opportunities for the support-service businessman! Imagine the number of new converts he could bring into the church. Imagine as he hired additional workers how he could disciple them and see their tithe help the local churches to become self-sufficient. (I better stop at this point. The last person who "imagined" this much was John Lennon and look what that got him!)

Truly, a number of concerns need to be addressed in the scope of today's world missions. First, believers need to be reminded that the Scripture says in I Corinthians 1:21 that God's strategy for battle is that *"...it pleased God by the foolishness of PREACHING to save them that believe."* (emphasis mine) Support services are fine, but when their budget consumes the funds that Biblically should be set aside for the preacher, then a serious problem arises.

The second concern is God's strategy of financing the war, is made clear in Romans 10:15 which says, *"...how shall they PREACH unless they be sent?"* (emphasis mine) Ten cents out of every $100 is not what He had in mind—I don't think.

Mission boards are now tripping over themselves asking churches to increase their giving to the missionaries because the value of the American dollar is not as strong as it once was. Having lived abroad as a missionary, I can well imagine how difficult that devaluation must be. But I wonder if it ever occurred to anyone that while the missionary may have to spend 15 percent of his income on food, his national church members are spending 70 percent or more of their income to feed their families because they earn much less, and they are not eating anywhere near the same standard as the missionary? Some are beginning to claim that the shrinking dollar will send many missionaries home. The truth is, however, that it is not a weak or a strong dollar that sends missionaries home; it is the lack of desire, burden, and motivation.

In 1900 nearly 100 percent of all missionaries were from North America and Europe, but today less than half are. Currently, more than 35 percent of all foreign missionaries are from Asia. They too have left their homes to go elsewhere in service—not as mechanics but as preachers. And yes, the weakened dollar does hurt them even though their support level, if they have support, is generally 1 percent of what their American counterpart receives. You see, when they go, they typically go as "tentmakers." They arrive on the field, find a job, and acquire their first converts from their workmates and neighbors. From that point, their churches grow.

The lack of funding can be devastating to the missionary. In America's churches, when funds are low, the pastor stands before the congregation, presents the needs, and passes the plate. Neither the missionary nor the national preacher has that luxury. Many people simply are not giving as they once did, and they are blaming the economy. Even the mighty Southern Baptist Convention woke to reality after reaching their missions' budget goal in 2008 of $300 million dollars when they heard the groundbreaking news that the "Grand Theft Auto IV" video game took in $310 million in sales on its first day of release! The SBC's entire annual offering was eclipsed by the sales of a secular video game in one day! Tragically, many of their members probably gave more for a game in one day than they did for souls in a year. And yet, they raised more money than all the other denominations in America! What does that say about the rest of us?

I have really been amazed at two totally opposite trends I am seeing in the United States.

(1) The number of good folks and churches that have decided that they can no longer support their chosen preacher or child because of their financial situation, and

(2) The number of folks and churches that have decided that they will continue to support their chosen preacher or child in spite of their financial situation and in spite of all the gloom and doom that is broadcast every day.

Just a few moments ago my son-in-law Michael was talking on the phone with a sponsor from Michigan. We had called him because the preacher he was supporting had failed to report, and when that happens, Final Frontiers recommends dropping support. *("No report, no support"; that's our policy.)*

In past years when such a call was made, about 95 percent of the sponsors would gladly take on another preacher in the place of the one let go. However, that number has now dropped to probably 50 percent. This particular sponsor shared with us that the company for which he works is tied in with GM and has been in Chapter 11 bankruptcy for over three years. Still he decided that by faith he would go ahead and take another preacher for support anyway.

I'm not a betting man (translation: I don't own stocks), but if I were, I would bet God will be taking very good care of him in the months ahead. After all, the infallible Word of God clearly says, *"He that giveth unto the poor shall not lack: but he that hideth his eyes shall have many a curse."* (Proverbs 28:27) Hmmm, curse or blessing, which one will I choose?

I do see a positive side. I see churches and families now being more careful in who and what they support. This carefulness is a natural reaction to having less to give. A millionaire may enjoy expensive caviar, but the average American clips the coupon out of the throw-away paper to save a quarter on a dozen eggs.

The same holds true in missions. When an abundance was available, money was thrown at the problem with the assumption that the problem would go away. That is precisely what has been done in the past with missions. Sadly, it became apparent that no matter how much money was given, the numbers of lost souls kept growing, and the missionary force kept shrinking. People who gave to missions grew discouraged and spent those funds on themselves instead.

Then came the spoilers—a handful who screamed "hold on"; and those spoilers have endeavored to open the eyes and hearts of American believers to an army of trained, but unknown, servants of God who are doing a crackerjack job (another Southern expression meaning "fantastic") of winning their own countrymen to Christ, planting churches, opening Bible colleges, and evangelizing the regions that have never had a Gospel witness. The problem is, those $100 bills just won't come toward missions. At best, missions receives ten cents out of those $100 bills, and at worse, one cent.

For some reason, my illustrating how saturated America is with the knowledge of the Gospel while others have never heard it has caused me to become a pariah to some, a traitor to others, and a whipping boy to a host of others. Do I love America? You bet I do! Do I care about souls in America? Of course I do.

I have done more than talk. I have started two churches in America—one in New York and one in California. I have won and seen thousands of converts baptized and trained a number of men who are in the ministry. I have confidence that I have done more than most in that area. But all that I have done does not change the fact that God's tithe is lavished on ourselves rather than obediently following His command. Believers are not fulfilling the Great Commission; to the contrary, they are guilty of perpetrating the Great Omission.

Let me illustrate my point from a well-known passage of Scripture of Jesus' feeding the five thousand. What if that story read a little differently? What if the disciples of Jesus chose to feed the 5,000 servings to the first 1,650 people sitting in front of Him and sent all the others home hungry? (The 1,650 out of 5,000 is 33 percent and equates to World C, which is 33 percent of the global population—that includes the American people.) Feeding the first 1,650 people would have been easier, required less work and less walking. Surely any friends and family they had were sitting up close. Surely because they were closer, they deserved to eat more than those in the back. And just because some were closer and had the opportunity to get a sack lunch doesn't mean they took it the first time it was offered. Maybe they weren't ready to eat, requiring the disciples of necessity to continually offer them food until they were finally ready for a snack. They had several chances to eat before the disciples finally walked all the way to the back. And besides, those people in the back looked different and smelled bad!

Wouldn't my version make for a strange story? I mean, how would you explain that one to the children in Sunday school? By the same token, what explanation for what they are doing or not doing will believers give when they stand before God someday?

If my version was the true story, it just wouldn't carry the same punch, even though the miracle would have been the same. After all, the miracle was not in the people's eating; it was in Jesus' taking the one basket of fish and bread, blessing it, and being able to feed not one small boy with the contents, but 5,000-plus people! Five loaves and two fishes fed all those present—not just those blessed to be close to the front. And the food did not run out until everyone had been fed!

"Foolish," you say. I agree. But my story is no more foolish than the way the Bread of Life is taken to the world today. He is not shared with the world; He is taken to the same countries and the same congregations over and over again, while ignoring the billions who live in nations and neighborhoods that have never heard His name. Even as billions are ignored, we as believers pat ourselves on the back and tell ourselves what a good job we are doing.

"You're wrong!" people say. (It won't be the first time.) Allow me then to conduct a little test. Let me list the names of a few countries and tell me whether or not you or your church supports missionaries there (and I probably do too personally, so there's nothing wrong with that):

- Do you or your church support "missionaries" in Australia, Canada, New Zealand, England, United States, Germany, Japan, South Korea?
- Do you or your church support "missionaries" to the US military, the prison, the youth?

Check ✓. Check ✓. Good for you (and me).

Next questions:

- Do you or your church support any missionaries in these countries: Syria, Egypt, Myanmar, Nepal, Congo, Thailand, Macedonia, Nepal, Belarus, Bangladesh, India, Pakistan, Afghanistan, Kazakhstan, Kyrgyzstan, Turkmenistan, Mustang, Bhutan, Yemen, Algeria, Cuba, Venezuela?
- Do you support "missionaries" to prisons, the military, the youth in any nations besides America?

Ooops! No checks here?

The first group of countries has a medium-to-high exposure or availability to the Gospel. In other words, if every American missionary was expelled from these countries, their own national churches would be strong enough to survive and also continue to expand without that missionary influence. They are among the nations receiving that whopping nine cents. (Now let's be good little nations and share!)

In the second group of countries, the Gospel is virtually unknown, missionaries are needed, and national preachers must be trained to reach their own. These are the nations where that one lonely penny is being expended—by choice.

Yes, these times of financial distress can be seen as days of gloom and despair, but only because that is how they are now affecting the way Americans live. What the American public needs to realize is that as far as missions is concerned, these times of financial difficulties are the only kind of days the rest of the world has ever known. God is affording Americans a brief opportunity in time to slightly experience the despair that most of the world has only and always known. It is time to face reality and stop being spoiled children. Americans cry because the float in their toilet tank is broken while 1.2 billion people in the world don't even have scrap wood with which to build an outhouse. If anything, this crisis in the American economy has taught us some important lessons on stewardship. People are paying down their credit cards at record rates, saving their money, and not spending. Many churches are no longer just giving to missions for the sake of giving; instead, they are carefully examining those to whom they are giving and why. For the first time, giving churches are demanding accountability and results from those they support. Well done!

One church in particular which has been struggling for years wrote to tell us that the current financial situation has overwhelmed them, and they have cut back to supporting only ten missionaries, but Final Frontiers is first on their list to keep supporting because of our results and accountability. They have not been alone in that remark. Final Frontiers has not waited until the crisis hit to demand accountability; that has been our ministry's watchword from day one. For nearly 25 years, we have held to a standard earning us a reputation of trust. In fact, even in these days of deficit, Final Frontiers' income for the support of national missionaries has grown by nearly 30 percent.

Temporary slump? Sure. Haven't you ever heard "what goes down must come up" or something like that? I don't believe this financial downward spiral is permanent. I don't know if it is a punishment or a natural ebb and flow of economy or just what it is. I do believe that it is a test and an opportunity from God for Christians to reveal to themselves and to Him where their priorities are and what is important to them. This is the question to ask ourselves: will we cut out luxuries to fund ministry, or will we cut out ministry to fund luxuries?

Those who have been spending their lives amassing wealth, storing it up, trusting in it even though Christ warned against doing so have now lost a great percentage of that wealth. This has provided many with a good opportunity to evaluate their disobedience and acknowledge that He was being kind when He admonished man to lay up treasures in Heaven rather than on earth (Matthew 6:19). As the economy returns to normalcy, the lesson God wants man to learn had best not be forgotten. Failing this test could mean having to take it all over again!

Personally, I like to look upon this period as a test; it's just one long S.A.T. (**s**uffering **a**nd **t**orture). When the Heavenly Teacher finally says "pencils down!" and things return to normal, I want to be able to know and remember that during this time of trial, I was *"...stedfast, unmoveable, always abounding in the work of the Lord"* and that "my labour" [the trials and discomforts of financial hardships] *is not in vain...."* (I Corinthians 15:58)

Years ago when I started Final Frontiers, I made a decision that as much as I could, I wanted to invest "my" money on that which will move when the trumpet blows. Brick and mortar, $10,000 steeples, $50,000 chandeliers, and $40,000 youth and senior vans will not move one millimeter when Christ returns. They will just be left sitting here for the use of the Antichrist. Obviously, having these kinds of things is not a sin, but having them at the exclusion of world evangelism, or using them as an excuse for not contributing to world evangelism, or using them to drain the coffers, thus permitting the abuse of these "necessities" to grow rather than financing world evangelism is a spiritual felony. I believe it is committing high treason against our King; it is a dereliction of our God-given duty.

Now don't get me wrong. In my office I enjoy air conditioning; I have a nice, comfortable, padded chair; I use computers and color printers; and on and on and on the list could go. Like you, I am human too. I want to be comfortable while I take up my cross each day and follow Him. And I really don't think that is a sin or in any way dishonors God. James 1:17 says, *"Every good gift...is from above* [Him]," and as I often tell people in churches where I speak, we should never apologize for the gifts God has given us nor feel guilty for having them.

But how tragic it is when God instructs believers to give His gift of eternal life to others, but they cannot afford to do so because they have spent all the money on themselves or they have gone so deeply into debt that they have become enslaved to their creditors. Indebtedness means they are now working for their creditors and not for Him.

Someone visited the United States years ago, and after he returned home, he was asked by his friends to describe Americans. He thought for a moment, then summarized us as "people who spend money they don't have to buy things they don't need to impress people they don't know."

What brought me to this point in my life was a conversation I had with an attorney friend in 1984. He was a believer, and we often talked and counseled with one another. He told me about a particular client he had acquired who had passed away. This client was a professing Christian, and he had left over $250,000 in his will for a charitable work. Therein lay the problem. You see, this man was born and reared in Pasadena, California, and he was concerned about hunger. He evidently enjoyed Thanksgiving and was saddened by the homeless people who did not get to enjoy such a meal, so he left his estate to provide Thanksgiving dinners for the homeless. Sounds noble enough. However, some problems arose which caused the estate to be in a perpetual state of limbo. You see, what he had not stipulated were the instructions on how to accomplish his goal.

- Who would feed the homeless people?
- How much of the estate could be used to pay for cooks and servers?
- Where would the homeless be fed?
- Could any homeless man come or only those living in Pasadena?
- Could someone from Pasadena who lived in Los Angeles ride over and get a meal?

On and on the questions continued. To be sure, that Christian gentleman meant well, but he did not exercise good sense in the establishment of his will. Often, those who still walk among the living don't do a much better job than he did.

- Have you ever added up how much money you pay on interest each month just on your credit card debts?
- What could believers alone accomplish for God if their interest payments were freed up to finance missions?
- Did you realize that $100,000 could give every citizen in some nations a copy of God's Word?
- Did you know that what is spent on a typical American church building could provide church facilities for 100, 200, or even more congregations in India?

On what do individuals and congregations spend their money? It would be a good exercise for every family to sit down and see just where their dollars are going. I think if you are like me, you will be quite surprised and ashamed.

Christians do so much in the name of Jesus that really

bears little resemblance to His character or actions. One of the greatest expenditures in American church budgets is our continual building programs. And let me hasten to say there is nothing wrong with having a building program. Churches are quick to declare they are building for the glory of God. Do they? If they do, then why does it seem they only want to be glorifying God with buildings that they get to personally inhabit during the week rather than glorify Him with buildings all over the country and world that they will never see or never enter?

❖

When I pastored in the Los Angeles area, it was common to see the larger, wealthy churches constantly erecting new buildings or remodeling existing ones. "All for the glory of God," they would say. But I was always bothered by the fact that none of these churches ever helped a sister church in the barrio remodel or build. They shared the same doctrine and the same denominational name, supported the same missionaries, and gave to the same causes. Why not help the younger, smaller, financially strapped congregations rather than just tearing down one barn to build a bigger barn?

Growing up in the South during the Civil Rights era brought forced integration into the schools some 20 years before it did in the North. As a result, in the 1960s and thereafter, the Christian school movement really gained momentum. Let's not kid ourselves. A large part of the momentum was to keep the white children separated from the black children. If that was, in fact, the motive, then so be it. But why claim then that it was a directive from God or even done for His glory? That claim was blatantly dishonest, and the kids who attended the Christian schools could see right through it.

To many, the building of gymnasiums or aerobic and weight rooms at their churches are done less as a ministry and more as a way to keep their kids away from the "undesirable" kids. In the end, the Gospel influence has been removed from the public schools and playgrounds as the Christian youth are isolated in a sterile Christian environment. It is not for me to determine if that is good or bad or the motives of why these things are done. That is the job of the Holy Spirit. I am just stating the obvious facts.

A money problem does exist, and because of it, some people will not get to go as missionaries because others do not give because of indebtedness, the lack of interest, the "what-I-see-I-want-and-what-I-want-I-get" philosophy, and waste. Frankly, I have never understood that reality, or I should say, I have never accepted it.

One great concern that I've heard about national preachers over the years is that if they are not paid, they won't work. I don't know who the "brain surgeon" was who initiated that bigoted statement, nor why he would run in such circles among such men of that caliber, or why after his years of ministry as a missionary (overseas pastor) that was the best he or his cohorts could produce. Certainly, the men with whom we work serve whether or not they're paid. In fact, that's one of the criteria for supporting them in the first place. Before they ever receive support, it is determined whether or not they deserve it because they have and are already serving in the capacity of a church planter.

But let's be honest and practice the old rule of "what's good for the goose is good for the gander." Suppose a missionary comes to your church and tells you he has a burden to go to point X on the globe. What he is saying is, "If I get enough support, I will go." The flip side of that statement is the always unspoken reality: "If I don't get enough support, I won't go."

Pastors, from how many missionaries have you ever received a letter saying,

Dear Pastor,
   I am sorry your church did not choose to support me. I wish you had. I was only able to raise 10 percent of my support. But I want you to know that I'm on the mission

field anyway. My family and I decided that this was God's will for us. So we borrowed money, purchased plane tickets, and we flew to country "x." Once we got here, I found out that I could get a job working at such-and-such factory (or on a banana plantation or whatever the case may be). So I'm working to provide for my family while I'm also planting a church. Just wanted to let you know where we are in case you're able to support us in the future.

When I pastored, I never received a letter like that. I have never yet had a pastor tell me that he has ever received such a letter. What we have received are letters that say,

Dear Pastor,
    For four years I've been on deputation, and I have only been able to raise 60 percent of my support. My wife and I have decided that it must not be the Lord's will for us to go. So I'm asking your church to please stop sending support to us. Thank you for all that you did to help us.
Sincerely,
John Doe, Missionary.

Oh my goodness! The thought that came to my mind the first time I read a letter like that was, "How did he misread God's will for his life?"

Then I wondered, "How did we misread that God wanted us to support him, seeing as he never even left the United States?"

Then I thought, "Are we supporting other men like him and we don't even know it yet?"

Then finally I wondered, "How much of our missions money did we give to this fellow who never went to the mission field?" Now, multiply that times who knows how many other churches that gave money to missionaries who never got to the mission field! It's a scary thought!

You really want to believe that those are rare occasions, but I fear that perhaps they are not. Boards compile statistics on how many missionaries quit after the first or second term as well as their reasons for quitting, but I have yet to come across an organization that has compiled a statistical analysis of how many of their qualified and approved missionaries started on deputation but never made it to the mission field. Why do you suppose boards don't keep records like that? I believe I can tell you why. It would be a discouragement beyond most people's capacity to bear, and so the facts are just swept under the rug.

These well-meaning servants quit during deputation though they carried the title of missionary with them for one year, or two years, or three years (six is the longest I have personally seen) as they proudly promoted their calling, their "game plan," and the mission board that had accepted them.

Often, boards are so eager to accept anyone who verbally says that God has called him to the mission field that all he needs for their acceptance is to submit a letter from his pastor and a signed doctrinal statement. Then the board adds two more missionaries (if he is married) to their growing list. Some boards have as many as one third of their "missionary" couples having yet to finish deputation, don't know the language of the people to whom they intend to minister, and have never even visited the field to which they claim to be called. The board calls them missionaries because of what they plan to do—not because of what they have done. Aren't you glad that Delta requires more from their candidates before they designate them as a pilot and put them in a cockpit?

The board should look for *quality* over *quantity*. If mission endeavors were operated as a business, that is precisely what would be done. It seems that the goal of many boards is to have more and more, whether it is money in the bank or missionaries on the field, as opposed to having better and better. Surely one excellent missionary can accomplish more than three or four nominal missionaries can accomplish. Because of the money issues, churches do not want to pour too much money into one person; instead, they want to keep it a level playing field.

Churches usually have a standard amount that is designated to each missionary. It doesn't matter if the missionary is 22 years old and never stepped foot on a foreign field or if he is 62 years old and has already planted 15 churches. Both men will receive the same amount of money. Unions are condemned because of that practice, but it is practiced with the missionary force without condemnation. Why is it done that way? Does the Bible teach that? No! I've yet to find a verse of Scripture that instructs how to mete out funds for missionaries.

I have been told that when mission boards began to rise up years ago, a learning curve had to be addressed. One of the concerns was what to pay the missionaries. They reasoned, "Surely someone living in Paris needed more finances than someone in an Amazon village."

Finally the question led to researching what a certain level of government employee was paid, depending on the country in which he lived, and emulating that pay scale. That's why someone going to the Ivory Coast asks for $6,000 a year while someone going to Japan asks for $9,000 a year. The problem is that the wages of a government employee are much higher than the average income of the country's citizens. The typical national pastor in the Ivory Coast would be delighted to receive $300 a month, and if he did, he would probably become the source of envy among his pastor friends.

American missionaries live and work among these people and earn 20, 50, 100 times more, while their supporting churches do not require even twice the amount of work or any amount of success. All we require from the missionaries our churches support is a letter once a month or once a quarter and agreement with any passing controversy that the pastor has championed. Why is it done that way? It is done that way because that is the way it has always been done. And that leads me to the next point.

Christianity Shift

- In 1800, 99 percent of the world's Christian population lived in Europe and North America, and 1 percent lived in the Global South.

- In 1900, 90 percent of the world's Christian population lived in Europe and North America, and 10 percent lived in the Global South.

- In 2008, 34 percent of the world's Christian population lived in Europe and North America, and 66 percent lived in the Global South

Mentality Problems

*Did you know that 500,000 villages
in India are waiting to hear a Gospel
presentation for the first time?*

The philosophies and mind-sets that hinder the fulfillment of the Great Commission can basically be divided into three categories:

- Those that keep the missionary from going
- Those that keep the missionary from going to the right places
- Those incorrect mind-sets that keep the missionary from being successful once he arrives

Mind-sets That Keep the Missionary From Going
❖

The "Charity-Begins-at-Home" Mind-set

I am sure that many readers who have read to this point are certain that I have lost my mind, but this is not what I am addressing. What I am referring to are the mind-sets that keep Christians from going and giving.

When I was a young missionary, one of my relatives made the comment that I shouldn't give my life to "those people" because they deserve to go to Hell or else they would already be Christians. What absurdity! Romans 10:14 addresses that concern: *"How then shall they call on him in whom they have not believed? and how shall they believe in him of whom they have not heard? and how shall they hear without a preacher?"* Why do "those people" deserve to go to Hell any more than I deserve to go to Hell? That idea is almost like a Christian karma: the philosophy of "those people haven't had the Gospel because they don't deserve the Gospel" implies that somehow some people did deserve it.

You would be surprised how typical, though disguised, this type of mentality is in fundamental churches. That's one reason why missions giving is so low and gets lower as the economy gets worse.

This relative rarely went to church, never tithed, lived with a cigarette between her fingers, and was trying to tell me I should not go into the entire world and preach the Gospel because America deserves the Gospel but the rest of the world doesn't. Her bigotry was cloaked in the concept that charity begins at home. Some entire denominations in the Baptist world have their own neighborhoods as their entire mission emphasis—not the world—simply because of the concept that charity begins at home. It is wrong! Charity began on the Cross, and believers were told to carry that charity to the whole world.

Others have the mentality of not going because they say missionaries' going doesn't accomplish any good since more missionaries have to be sent, generation after generation. In the early 1990s, the parliament of Thailand passed a law that would take effect in the year 2000. Fortunately, the law was later rescinded, but what the government officials had in mind was to expel all the foreign missionaries beginning in the year 2000. The country was not enacting this law out of hatred for Christianity or from a fear that their national identity as a Buddhist nation would be lost. Rather, they determined that around the year 2000, Christian missionaries would have been serving in Thailand for 200 years. (One of the first was the son of William Carey.) If after 200 years of work, the Thai people had not embraced Christianity to the point that it had assimilated into their culture and if their own Thai pastors did not have the ability to propagate it without outside intervention, then Christianity was just not meant for the Thai. In short, it had failed because it was not accepted by the people but was still seen as a Western religion. Thank the Lord this ruling was overturned.

There are many reasons why missionaries must continue to go to the same countries. Preeminent among them is the fact that many geographical territories are comprised of ethnic groups that live within them. Where one ethic group may have heard the Gospel and have been saturated with the Gospel, the others have not heard or may have only had a slight taste of it. Therefore, more missionaries need to be supported until all have heard the Gospel. But the "missionary" does not have to be an American. He could be one of their own citizens. He is not a missionary because of where he is from but rather to where he is going, and he is going to reach those who have never before heard the Gospel.

The "Give-a-Man-a-Fish..." Mind-set

Others, though well-meaning, repeat a proverb so overused that its validity seems to be without question. This proverb has become almost Biblical in status—as if the very hand of God inscribed it on the tablets of Moses. I get so tired of hearing people repeat the old axiom of "give a man a fish, and you feed him for a day; teach him how to fish, and you feed him for a lifetime." I have yet to hear someone say it who has ever actually given a man a fish. This axiom is nothing more than a politically correct way of excusing oneself for not doing what God has called him to do.

The idea of giving a man a fish and feeding him for a day implies that doing so is wrong. Christians tend to forget that Jesus did it for 5,000 men on one occasion and 4,000 on another.

To these people I would say, remind me when you don't have a job, when you're struggling, when your children are going to bed hungry because I will be inclined to help you out. So remind me not to give you that fish for a day. I think you'll feel differently about quoting that proverb then. You'll be looking for a net of fish!

Give them a fish; you feed them for a day. Teach them how to fish; you feed them for a lifetime. Oh, really? If you teach a man how to fly, will he fly for a lifetime? Not unless he can afford to rent or buy a plane! If you teach a man to play football, will he play football for a lifetime? Not unless he has got a good doctor and excellent health insurance!

Just because you teach a man to fish, it doesn't mean he will automatically be fed for a lifetime. What if he doesn't own a fishing pole? What if he doesn't have a line or a hook? What if he's nowhere near a river to be able to fish in the first place? What if a drought dries up the lake? I know that is not what the ditty is saying, but I also know how the ditty is abused.

Today in evangelical circles, the idea is being propagated that if a man is given a fish for one day, his dignity is destroyed. I can take you all over the world and show you men who could care less about their dignity. They are hungry. Search the Internet under the keyword "starvation," and you will find photos of a hungry, dying child squatting in the wilderness with a vulture not ten feet away literally waiting for that child to die so that he can be eaten. You will see a picture of a man so hungry that he is eating cow dung from the anus of the beast in an effort to stay alive. Observe the living conditions of people like that and then talk to me about dignity.

The "That's-Not-the-Way-It's-Always-Been-Done" Mind-set

To me the mother of all mentality problems is the absurd statement, "That's not the way it's always been done." True. Unfortunate, but true. The method of missions which I am suggesting has not always been done. However, missions were originally done this way. The American people got away from this Biblical method first by doing no missions and then by attempting to do it in an illogical manner. Of course, even an illogical method is better than nothing. All I am suggesting is a return to the Biblical pattern of missions, which doesn't necessarily mean sending someone who looks like me to preach to people who don't look like me.

It is true that the way Final Frontiers is doing missions today is not the way it has always been done—though it is the way it was first done. There's no rule above the door that says missions must be done the way it has always been done. In fact, if there was, that plaque should be ripped down and rewritten to say, "It's best not do missions the way it's always been done." There are 124 million births each year, but Christianity's 4,000 missions agencies report baptizing only 4 million people a year. Does it look to you like doing missions the way it has always been done is productive?

The truth is, very little is still done the way it's always been done. How many horses and buggies are parked outside of modern churches? After Sunday night services, do you have to be concerned about where you step? Are the bathrooms located out back of the church? No, of course not. When you step into the church and flip a switch, the lights instantly come on. There's heat; air conditioning; cushioned seats; carpet; an indoor, heated baptistery; and microphones. Is that the way it has always been done?

I can remember in Atlanta in the 1960s when churches would advertize in the Saturday paper on the church page that there was air conditioning in their auditorium. The reasoning was to attract visitors to their church using this "modern" invention. (These were only summer advertisements of course.) Oh, some of the sermons that were preached on "modernism" and "compromise" included diatribes about the evils of air conditioning and how weak was the faith of those who would let such a contraption dictate where they would go to church. The sermons were legion until one by one all churches could afford to install an air-conditioning system, and then they too changed their Saturday church page advertisement. Who could blame them!

As a young boy growing up in the town of Wadley, Georgia, my father had a unique job. Every Sunday morning he would go the basement of the Methodist church and load up the furnace with coal so that the auditorium would be warm by the time the church members arrived. I don't think anybody has that job in America's churches today. Churches have PA systems, pianos, organs, climate-controlled auditoriums, and padded seats. Some churches even have recorded music. Some churches used song books, but now many don't even own them; instead they display the words of the songs on the walls through projection systems. This was yet another "pagan" invasion of modernism into American churches—until of course we could all afford to have a video projector.

When the average family goes home next Sunday after church, the wife will walk into the kitchen and open a big white box. Out of that box, she will take out a smaller cardboard box. After opening the little box, she will put that little box into a bigger metal and glass box. She will then turn a knob or press a few buttons, and in two or three minutes, the little box comes out piping hot. She will put it on the table, and the whole family will all gather around, pray, eat the contents, and enjoy their meal.

When the dinner's over, she'll collect the plates and glasses, and she will put them in another box, push a button, and presto, they will get washed.

Now if you had prophesied to your grandmother about those kind of conveniences being available someday, she would have thought you were a witch. My point is this: Very little of anything is done the way it's always been done. So why should Christians insist on doing God's work the way it's always been done? That philosophy is wrong, and it shows that Christians do not have the proper heart of a steward, or a servant, or a slave. To think of doing the Saviour's work in such a slipshod, antiquated manner when everything else is done as scientifically and technologically advanced as possible should be shameful to us. This shows where the heart and mind of many a Christian truly is.

❖

The "American-Money-Belongs-to-American-Missionaries" Mind-set

Another disturbing mentality that defeats the goal of involving more churches in missionary support is the belief that "American money belongs to American missionaries." I particularly have a great deal of fun with this anti-Biblical misconception. My first question is always, "Where in the Bible do you read the term, 'American' money?" Of course, it's not there. Psalm 24:1 states *"The earth is the LORD's and the fulness thereof...."* May I paraphrase that verse? Everything on this planet belongs to God. It doesn't belong to me, to a certain church, or to a certain denomination, and it surely doesn't belong to the United States of America. Since it belongs to God, it should therefore be used to accomplish God's purposes.

The Great Commission was not written to the United States churches, or to the British churches, or to the Italian churches. It was written to all churches and demanded that the body of Christ is to go into the entire world and preach the Gospel to all people. No country is excluded; therefore, the command is not inclusive to any one country. If it were, then it could be said that "American money belongs to American missionaries." Since it isn't, it must be said that God's money belongs to God's missionaries. Obviously, the proper steward will want to find the most qualified, competent missionary he can in whom to invest God's money.

When you go out to buy a new car for your teenage daughter or son, do you buy the cheapest one you can find? Well, maybe... But you also want to find the safest car you can find. When you buy them winter clothes, do you look for something that is adequate or something that will keep them warm? For those whom you love, you always try to do the best you can. Should God's work not be done in the same way?

❖

*The "If-You-Give-Them-Money, You-Will-Ruin-Them
and-the-You-Can't-Trust-Them" Mind-set*

If I give money to a veteran national preacher, it will ruin
him, but if I give money to a brand-new, novice, or even veteran
American missionary, it will not ruin him? Is it not bigotry to
say that one's nationality will keep him honest, or is it just that
no one wants to believe that a white man can be ruined by
money, but a brown man or a black man will—not could, but
will—be. I seem to remember a verse of warning in Matthew 7:1,
"Judge not, that ye be not judged." Over $22 billion is lost in
our churches each year due to ecclesiastical crimes. Obviously,
some of us "white boys" aren't too honest either.

Can someone please explain these questions to me? Now I
know what you are going to say, "The $100 you give to an Amer-
ican missionary really is a drop in the bucket to what he really
gets, so it's not really going to affect him. But the same $100
going to a national preacher could be his entire monthly salary.
So, yes, he will be affected." If that is your answer, then you have
just proven my point. If giving $100 to an American missionary
means nothing to him, then why give it to him? Why not give it
to someone to whom it will mean a world of difference?

I am not suggesting paying a full salary to the national
preachers; and on the same token, I am not suggesting paying
a full salary to the American missionaries either. "What's good
for the goose is good for the gander," my father used to say. If
the national preacher is expected to work as well as to receive
some support for his ministry, then so should the American
missionary be expected and even demanded to work while he's
receiving some compensation for his ministry. But I will further
address that subject in a later chapter because contrary to
what Christians have been told, it is not illegal for an American
missionary to receive a paycheck from his church.

The Moravian missionaries were examples for all of us to follow. They never practiced the art of deputation; they simply

went where God led them and carried the tools of their trade with them (just as William Carey did). They worked with their hands while they "missionaried"—just as Paul did. And when in the Caribbean they were denied access to the slaves living on sugar the plantations, some sold themselves as slaves and lived in slave quarters in order to be able to reach those for whom God had burdened them.

This idea of "ruining them" has led to national believers being referred to as "rice Christians," meaning they will serve as long as they are being fed. But when their salary is cut off, they will quit the serving. I am sure that might be right in some cases, but it has nothing to do with their nationality and all to do with their character. Besides, how many times have you heard of a missionary who lost his entire support but stayed on the field anyway? Never.

To me, this philosophy is extremely insulting. I know and have known hundreds of national Christians who have suffered for the name of Christ. They have buried their children; endured beatings, mutilations, and burning; have been shot, stabbed, and thrown off rooftops; starved; and been deprived of clothing. They have seen their wives raped, their sons decapitated or taken from them to be slaves. These men served faithfully before they had ever seen a dollar, and then some dare label them as rice Christians! These are men of whom the world is not worthy! As the old hymn states, these are men who have "fought to win the prize and sailed thro' bloody seas." Those who revile them in the name of Christ have never suffered, rarely sacrificed, and will be "carried to the skies on flow'ry beds of ease."

Shortly after starting Final Frontiers, I was chided by the president of a certain fundamental, independent Baptist mission board. He told me in no uncertain terms that supporting the nationals was wrong because they could not be trusted. He knew they were untrustworthy for a fact because the ministry he led had begun by supporting nationals and had to switch canoes in the middle of the river. Allow me to share in my own words what he related to me.

> Several of us had gone to ___ (a certain Caribbean island) to hold a crusade. That week hundreds came to our meetings, and many were converted. Since we were all pastors and had to return home, we needed to find someone who could start a church and pastor these people. We decided to place an ad in the local paper and asked for those to apply who were interested in being a pastor and were willing to work for us. Many men applied, and we selected the one who we felt most qualified. We returned home and began to send thousands of dollars for Bibles, tracts, the erection of a church facility, and his salary. About a year or so later, we went back, and to our surprise, there was no church, no buildings, and no Bibles. Instead this man had bought cars and built himself a beautiful house. You see, Jon, you cannot trust the nationals.

I was much younger than he was, and I wanted to season my response with grace. I felt that I had to point out to him that the error was not with the national preacher; it was the American pastors who had broken the principles of God's order for appointing pastors for the church.

- First, the instruction in I Timothy 5:22 says to lay hands on no man suddenly. They rushed to appoint a pastor.
- Second, I Thessalonians 5:12 says to know them which labor among you in the Lord. They hired a man they did not even know.
- Third, I Timothy 3:7 says that a pastor should be a man of good report and not serving for financial gain as commanded in I Peter 5:2.

Instead of observing these commands, they hired a bad man who responded because a newspaper carried an ad for a salaried position.

The truth is, many men will gladly wear the disguise of a pastor if the money is right. But to state that it is common among foreigners and imply that such a thing never happens in the United States is hypocrisy. After all, all pastors are national pastors.

Final Frontiers is very careful to fully investigate the preacher before becoming involved in supporting him. In essence, we do our homework up front so that we are not embarrassed later. I will share more on that matter in another chapter.

The "Complacency" Mind-set

One of the greatest hazards to world conquest for Christ is the complacency of the typical Christian. It's amazing how many Christians can quote batting averages, television schedules, and the top ten movies but can scarcely quote a verse of Scripture. If God's Word was taken away, as it has been from numerous cultures throughout history, how many passages would the average Christian carry in his heart? Complacency is a cancer that eats at the very soul of one's faith.

Around 2004 I stopped by a Christian bookstore in the area. I wandered through its many aisles of self-help books that overwhelmed me with how to be a better Christian father, a better Christian husband, a better Christian employee, and certainly, how to be a better Christian. If my wallet had been deep enough, I could have walked out with enough trinkets to fill a department store at Christmastime. The trinkets included Christian bumper stickers, Christian bookmarks, Christian mugs, Christian fine china, Christian plaques, Christian lapel pins, Christian T-shirts, Christian pencils, and even a Christian doormat with the ever-present outline of the Christian fish. (That symbol was supposedly used by the early church for one secret believer to recognize another one, yet in reality was not "invented" until the fourth century.) How incredible! Only in today's culture could people think to make money by inducing believers to wipe off the mud of the world on a symbol of Christ before entering Christian houses. What in the world could have been the motivation for such a product? In a word, profit. I was overwhelmed by all I saw, and to be honest, I was wondering just how much of it I could take home with me. Many items were beautiful and, in many cases, uplifted my spirit with their words of praise.

As I progressed on my exploration looking for certain CDs, I decided to take a look at the "Missions" section. After all, missions is the life-blood of the church. God never commanded man to go into all the world and build Christian bookstores in every nation. He was not told to build hospitals, Bible colleges, etc. All of these are good (and needed), but none are the fulfillment of the Great Commission; rather, they are the result of it. They are peripheral—the evidence of our abundance of wealth and ingenuity. If there ever was a case of putting the cart before the horse, American Christians have mastered it.

Cutting my way through the foliage of merchandise that was choking this jungle of Christianity into which I had entered, I was having difficulty in finding the "Missions" section. "Ah," I thought, "a native guide employed here can surely help me." So after waiting patiently for others to be assisted, I asked, "Where is your missions section?" The first few seconds of silence seemed to be minutes, and I felt awkward. It was obvious that my question had never before been asked of her. I became as stunned by her silence as she was by my inquiry. Then suddenly the puzzled look on her face shocked me back into reality. I hadn't been in a Christian bookstore in years, and suddenly I was remembering. It all came back to me in that look! In almost every store I have ever visited, I have gotten the same puzzled look when I ask for books on missions. It is almost as if they don't exist. Maybe that's the problem. And if they don't exist, why don't they? Is it that no one writes about missions or that no one wants to read about missions?

As the puzzled employee uttered the customary "hmms," I thought to myself, "Surely there is a book here on William Carey or Adoniram Judson or Jonathan Goforth." As I was reasoning this all out in my mind, the light bulb flashed on over her head, and she said, "We do have some things back here; follow me." (On the way, she stopped to ask a senior employee where the section was—just to be sure I suppose.) We walked literally to the furthest corner of the store to one little ten-foot long aisle. Here at long last was the alleged "missions section." There were no world maps showing where the unreached people live. There were no CDs of missions music. (Could this be because there has been virtually none written?) There were no missionary biographies—not even a single book on Lottie Moon, and this was a Southern Baptist bookstore. There were not even any how-to books on holding a missions conference or coloring books or pens or bookmarks or doormats. It seems that missions has become the religious dodo bird of this generation. We've all heard of it, but does it still exist? Did it ever?

In 1986 when starting Final Frontiers, I received a publication from a mail-order bookstore that boasted on its front cover that over 10,000 titles of books could be ordered from that catalog. I looked through the entire publication and not one single title of a missions book was listed. Not one out of 10,000! Eighteen years had passed at that time, and nothing had changed.

Before you think I am too hard on bookstore owners, let me stop to say that I have a basic grasp of marketing—supply and demand. (I told you it was basic.) I understand that the owners will not spend money to stock their shelves with books that no one will buy. The fault is not theirs; it is the fault of Christians. If the typical Christian cared about missions, the shelves would be overflowing with products. Most Christians just do not care, and that, my friend, is why the world still does not know the name of Jesus.

Since I have been speaking on missions for the past 25 years, I have often had to share the pulpit with others. Many have been the times that a singing group was at the church the same time I was. Typically, they are given 45 minutes to an hour to sing and entertain the congregation. I am given five minutes to talk about missions. This was specifically because the pastor did not want the "challenge" I was to give to interfere with their time of singing.

At one church in the Atlanta, Georgia, area, I recall that at the end of the service, a "love offering" was taken. When I left that day after the service, the pastor gave me a check for $25 and proudly announced that they had raised and given more than $6,000 to the singing group. Oh well, somebody had to pay for the bus in which they were traveling, but who was going to pay to get the Gospel to more than two billion people who still have not heard it?

Christians care too much about themselves, their desires, their needs, and their pleasures; they spend "God's tithe" to build "bigger barns" for themselves. And let's not kid ourselves either; none of those items are for God. He does not need a family life center, a bowling alley, a weight room, or an aerobics area; but then again, God doesn't need padded pews, air conditioning, or indoor baptisteries. None of these luxuries are wrong, none are evil, but neither are they ultimately necessary. What is necessary is reaching the lost with the Gospel.

I realize that these "tools" can be instruments that open the door of opportunity to witnessing to others, but come on, knocking on doors can do the same thing. Who is going to pay to open the doors of opportunity to reaching the world?

As I have already stated, what perplexed me as a pastor years ago is how God's people will give to build a new auditorium or classrooms for their church, but they generally won't give a dime to build one for another church of like faith in their own town that just happens to be down the block or in the ghetto.

Who are we kidding? We are not building to the glory of God; we are building to the comfort of His spoiled children. We say we are giving to God, but in reality, we are giving to ourselves, to our comfort, to our own children's youth programs. If we were truly giving to God, we would be more concerned about where money is given and how it is used. We pay for padded pews so that our oversized bottoms will be comfortable while we sing "Send the Light"; then we give precious little to send it. We spend $10,000, $50,000, $200,000 on an air-conditioning system so that we remain comfortable for those three hours a week we use the auditorium. And then we proclaim that our churches cannot afford to take on any more missionary projects. These men whom we are failing are dying from heat exhaustion while we complain that the thermostat is turned down too low.

Churches and ministries will borrow money to build structures, but would never consider doing so to support missions. Why is that? It is time for shepherds to stand before their congregations and rebuke them for their complacency. Church members don't need to be patted on the back and told that their complacency is acceptable to God. Church members need to be swatted on the seat of their pants and told to repent and do what God put them here to do for Him and not just for themselves.

As I said, complacency is like a cancer. At first Christians don't even know it is growing inside them, but in time it weakens them, makes them ineffective, and eventually destroys them. That is why God warned in I John 2:15a, *"Love not the world, neither the things that are in the world."* As His children, believers should love the things that He loves. If believers spend enough time with Him, they will become more like Him. They will love the things He loves and despise the things He despises. This is as much a law of nature as gravity is.

I am very much like my father was, and my son Daniel is very much like me. I don't wonder why. It doesn't surprise me. I expect this, and God expects His children to be like Him.

We preach this as if it is something we must do or give up to accomplish. That is not the case; this should involve no effort at all on our part. If our hearts are in love with Him, it is natural to want to be like Him, to gravitate to what He likes, and to shun what He dislikes. At first this may be just an effort to please Him, but before long, the effort will be replaced with a sincere desire. When a person's heart is conformed to the image of Christ, his likes and dislikes are transformed too. A person will never live right just because of preaching. Help the people to fall in love with Jesus, and those people cannot be stopped from living right.

Mind-sets That Tell a Missionary Where to Go and Not to Go

The "Sprinkling-the-Nations" Mind-set

It was prophesied in the book of Isaiah that our Lord would "sprinkle the nations"—not that He would submerse them, but that He would sprinkle the nations. Truthfully, that's what missions work is really all about—sending a man to "sprinkle" an area that has not been exposed to the Gospel. If this missionary has done his job efficiently and in a Biblical manner, he would leave behind or call up someone who will plant a church there or solidify that church as he moves on to sprinkle the next area.

Then the evangelist, the prophet (preacher/expositor), the pastor, and the shepherd will come in, and what began as a sprinkling will become a deluge. What began as a sprinkling will become knee deep, covering that area in the knowledge of the glory of the Lord! All the while, the missionary continues to move on to the next work.

The problem is that the missionaries have not been taught to function in that way. They have been taught to go and stay. As a general rule, a missionary does not move on to another place or country, but if he does, he must first call the home office and ask them to send another missionary to take his place. That describes the modern concept of missions, but Biblically, that is not missions work; rather, it is pastoring in another land—albeit unsuccessfully pastoring.

Nothing is wrong with this concept other than the fact that any true missionary should have been able to train a national pastor to take his place after years of service with a single congregation. (But then so should every American pastor.) God bless these men of God for what they have done and for their sacrifice and willingness to live cross-culturally. God bless them. However, pastoring is not doing missionary work unless these leaders are using that church as a hub of a wheel from whence they go out and plant more churches all over the area. That's missionary work—a church planting another church.

But unfortunately, today's missionaries are not trained to do that. Men have gone to a foreign field and started a church and are still there—5 years later, 10 years later, 15 years later, and even 20 years later. It's time to retire, and they are still in the same area, and what do they do? They call another missionary from their home office to come and take their place because they are retiring. These mind-sets are disruptive to missions. Too many missionaries act as if God calls them only to a specific place rather than to a people and to a select people, rather than to all people.

The "People-Don't-Live-Where-They-Are-Supposed-to-Live, or-do-they?" Mind-set

Take India, for example. More and more people today are supposedly being called as missionaries to India. In fact, it's becoming somewhat of a fad. And I am glad that people have a burden and a heart to reach the Indians. They need to be reached. But it is becoming very difficult to receive a visa as a missionary to India. I won't say impossible, but next to it. But, my question is, did God really call that person to go to the geographical nation of India or to the ethnic peoples of India? And of course, India is comprised of thousands of ethnic groups.

Let me explain this in this way. Let's suppose you have a burden in your heart to go to India, but you cannot go because you just cannot get in. What about the South Pacific instead? Could you go there?

You say, "Oh, but God didn't call me there. God called me to India."

Did He? Did He call you to India, or did He call you to the Indians? Did you know that 37 percent of the people who live in the nation of Fiji are Indian? Did you know that some nations in South America and the Caribbean are highly populated with Indians? So if your call is to go to India to reach the Indians, you don't have to go to India. All you have to do is go to some place where Indians reside.

Pockets of Indians can be found living in New York, Atlanta, Dallas, Chicago, Los Angeles, Denver, or Seattle. Like all ethnic groups, Indians live all over the world. In fact Nepal, Thailand, Guyana, Mauritius, Trinidad, Tobago, United Arab Emirates, Suriname, and Fiji are some countries where the Hindu or Indian population accounts for about 20 percent of the total national population. Those who want to reach the world for Christ need to start thinking about reaching the people of the world from the standpoint of ethnic groups—not as geographical boundaries.

The "You-Can't-Go-There-as-a-Missionary" Mind-set

Another destructive mind-set is telling someone he "can't go there," meaning the missionary cannot go to that particular country as a missionary. While it's true that many of the world's countries are either closed or highly restricted to missionaries today, that doesn't automatically mean one can't live in and minister in them. It just means a person cannot officially go there as a missionary.

This is the next question: "But I thought you were opposed to someone's going as a teacher."

No, I never said that. What I said was that I am opposed to calling a school teacher a missionary, just like I would be opposed to calling a primary girls' Sunday school class teacher a pastor. She is not a pastor; she is a teacher. The same differ-ence exists for a missionary as well. Just because a missionary teaches does not mean that that teaching is his profession. And just because a teacher goes to another country does not make him a missionary.

My mother was a teacher for decades. I was a teacher. Are you telling me that if I teach in Georgia, I'm a teacher, but if I teach in Mexico, I'm a missionary? I'm teaching the same classes—grammar or science or mathematics or even a Bible class. But because I cross over a national boundary, I'm now a missionary? That thinking is just absurd. I feel there is ab-solutely nothing wrong with a missionary's being a teacher; it may even be prudent or necessary. However, plenty is wrong with a teacher's calling himself a missionary or being supported as one—just because he teaches outside of his homeland.

That does not mean that a missionary cannot teach classes or do repairs on an airplane engine, etc. Many good ministries are involved in aviation, and more are probably needed. I am not opposed to them, and even if I were, so what? Who am I? I just don't believe other professionals should be supported as missionaries. Find another way to support them. I don't suggest not supporting them; I am merely suggesting that another way be found to support them.

May I share a scenario that I think anyone who has lived overseas for any length of time at all would have a hard time disagreeing with? Currently, the way an airplane mechanic goes abroad is to raise support as a missionary so he can go to a cer-tain country and work on the airplanes that are owned by the mission board or the missionaries. The support being given to the airplane mechanic is actually draining the missionary funds in American churches. Let me share another scenario to con-sider. Move that same mechanic to that same country, and let him work in that same hangar as an independent businessman with a valid work visa or residency. In other words, he can go to that country and legally open his own business of repairing planes and airplane engines. He does it for a fee—just as he would in the United States and just as every other mechanic in that country has done or is doing.

But some would say, "It's not right to charge the missionaries."

Why is it wrong to charge missionaries? They have to pay for their groceries, their gasoline, and car repair. Why should they not pay to get their planes worked on?

But for the sake of argument, let's say you are right and that you shouldn't charge missionaries. It's a simple solution. The airplane mechanic charges everyone else for whom he works, but then he does the work for the missionaries for free.

If you have ever lived in a foreign country, I think you would agree with my opinion as follows: if you are living in any country and you are wealthy enough to own an airplane that needs some repair, you would much rather pay a certified American engine mechanic to work on it than pay someone from your own country who apprenticed with somebody else who apprenticed with somebody else.

The truth of the matter is, this airplane mechanic could be working on the planes owned by the government and business leaders in that country. As such, he could be getting to know those people and having an opportunity to witness to them. At the same time, with the surplus he is making because it won't cost so much to live in that country, he could now afford to work on the missionary's airplane engines free of charge. What has that done?

- One, he has a legitimate tax deduction for his income taxes this year.
- Two, he is respectable in his community as people find out how much of his time and income he donates to the Lord's work.
- Three, he now has the opportunity to witness to people he never would have been able to witness to before.
- Four, he will probably enjoy an even higher standard of

living, allowing him more money to tithe to the local churches there.

- Five, he will still accomplish what he went there to do, while at the same time freeing missionary support money for bona fide, proven, experienced missionaries.

I have been accused of being anti-missionary; that's about as ridiculous as accusing a smoke alarm salesman of being anti-firemen. His purpose and goal is not to put the firemen out of work but to save the lives of people by alerting them of the fire. When the firemen arrive, they can spend their time on putting out the flames before they spread through the neighborhood, rather than on saving lives. I remind you again that I am a missionary.

My point is this: my goal is to reach the world with the Gospel of Christ. I am looking for every place to cut back expenditures in order to move forward rapidly and effectively to accomplish that goal of reaching the world. Because of the current economy, family budgets, business budgets, and church budgets have, of necessity, been trimmed. The economy for missions has always been bad, but even so, the need to reduce exists there as well. What can be cut back? The answer is simple: cut whatever is not essential and whatever can be funded through another source so that the remaining monies are used purely for the purpose of doing missions work.

To those who say "I can't go there," I have another question: "Why can't you go there?" True, you are not allowed to go as a missionary. So then, go as a barber. In a year, learn how to cut hair, get certified, move to that country of choice, and open up a barber shop. "A year?" you say. "That's a waste of time."

Really? And four years of deputation isn't? When you arrive in your "adopted" country, do something that will be unlike any other barber shop there. Advertise it. Advertise, "Come to the American barbershop. Let an American cut your hair." Print up flyers and pass them out on street corners, in the mall parking garages, and in the city's business district. Pay kids to pass

them out. Do you know what will happen? People will come to
let you cut their hair because they have never before had their
hair cut by an American. They want to see what kind of job an
American does. Guess what? They will want to practice their
English on you while they're there. Some of them might be so
ego-driven that they will have you cut their hair so their friends
can see them being served by an American. They want to be
able to tell an American what to do! "Cut it this way. Cut it that
way. You're cutting too much"—whatever the case may be.

The truth of the matter is, you will have the most prominent
people in the community—doctors, lawyers, police chiefs, politicians, military colonels—coming to you to get their hair cut.
Why? Simply so they can say, "The American cuts my hair." And
while a client is sitting in your chair, wrap that hot towel around
his face, lean him back in the chair, pull out the strap, begin to
sharpen that razor blade, place it gently on his neck, and ask,
"If you were to die today, do you know for sure you would go to
Heaven?" Just kidding on that one! I wouldn't recommend it.

My point is this: when these men come and sit in your chair
for you to cut their hair, you have a ten-or fifteen-minute opportunity to tell them who you are, why you are there, how
much you love their country, how you gave up your own home
and your own culture and your own life to come there and live
among them and to be one of them. Why? Because you're concerned about their souls and you are concerned about their
dying and going to Hell without the knowledge of Jesus Christ,
the Son of God.

As they come back every few weeks, you can talk with them
more. Give them a tract and give a New Testament to read. Before too long, Mr. Barber, you have started a church! And you
are beginning to fill up the churches in your area with good
men who have been born again and who have the ability to tithe
and finance the ministry in their own countries. No, you can't
go everywhere as a missionary, but that surely doesn't mean
you can't go somewhere.

You say, "Well, I knocked on the front door of the country, and they wouldn't let me in."

Then go to the back door and see if you can't get in there!

"I knocked on the back door, and they wouldn't let me in."

Well then, my advice is to check the windows. One of them is bound to be unlocked, so crawl through. And if you still can't find a way in, then that's what rocks are for! Break a window and crawl in anyway. If God called you to go to that country, you don't have a right to let anything keep you from going there.

❖

The "10/40-Window-and-the-Rest-of-the-House" Mind-set

In 1974 at the first Lausane Conference, a missions philosophy was introduced that was definitely needed. It was the desire to encourage the missionary—the sending churches were to emphasize the conversion of the lost by targeting those ethnic groups that had never had exposure to the Gospel, clearly more than a billion souls.

Research indicated that the majority of those "people groups" lived between the tenth and fortieth latitudes; thus, the movement became known as "The 10/40 Window." This was, without a doubt, a momentous moment in the cause of world evangelism and taking the Gospel to the whole world. The only problem that has arisen is that some churches now give so much emphasis to this window that they have forgotten about "the rest of the house."

While it is true that the majority of the unreached peoples live in the 10/40 window, millions of others live elsewhere and should not be abandoned. Final Frontiers has not targeted that Window, but because our ministry seeks to take the Gospel to the final frontiers that have not yet been reached, our ministry therefore supports more national preachers there than in the rest of the world combined. Still, we don't forget about the rest of the world by putting all our eggs in one basket.

Just as it would be wrong to fail to witness to America's neighbors because America already has the Gospel, so it is also wrong to ignore nations and ethnic groups because their inhabitants do not live within a certain geographical latitude.

Mind-sets That Keep a Missionary From Succeeding Once He Arrives

It is always wonderful when a missionary and his family finally arrive at his chosen field of service. Expectations are high, the children are excited to make new friends, and the task of setting up the house is eagerly commenced by the wife. But after the novelty wears off and reality is served with a scoop of discouragement on top, some are as eager to leave the field as they were to get there in the first place. More often than not, from the husband's point of view, this desire to leave the ministry is due to discouragement. His two primary concerns revolve around the following: "I'm not doing what I came here to do" or "I'm not having the results I expected to have." If these issues can be resolved, there will be a higher retention rate among missionaries. Statistics show that of the missionaries who make it through deputation, reach the field, stay a full term, and come home for their first furlough, over 55 percent of them will never return to the field. Why is this consistently happening?

❖

The "We-Keep-Repeating-the-Same-Unproductive-Methods-Used-by-Those-Who-Preceded-Them" Mind-set

The first mind-set is for the missionaries to keep doing the same type of unproductive work that had been done before their arrival. So much of what I am addressing seems to be pure common sense to a businessman. Unfortunately, I am not just addressing business people: I am also addressing those in the religious world.

For whatever reason, people seem to lock into a pattern of doing things a certain way, and they never seem to break out of it. Missionaries tend to look at those who went before them and assume that the methods those previous missionaries used will work today, but that is not necessarily the case. Missionaries must be willing to be innovative.

I wouldn't recommend that anyone emulate the methods of a missionary who has been on his field of service for 5 years and still has a church averaging 15 people. Preaching his sermons and talking about the same Saviour are acceptable, but don't use the methods he has been using because his methods obviously are not working. They are not productive, and most of the methods that I have seen around the world are not very productive. Missionaries need to forsake these unproductive methods.

❖

The "Compounds-Vs.-Communities" Mind-set

Missionaries tend to live in compounds instead of communities. In other words, they look for a place where they can all be neighbors with one another never having to step outside the confines of the protective wall. How ridiculous and how absurd! That is not how missionaries learn to communicate with the people. They need to have them as next-door neighbors. The missionary needs to be accessible to the little boy who comes and says, "Can I cut your grass?" or "Can I wash your car?" or whatever the case may be. The missionary's children need the opportunity to play with and learn from the children in the neighborhood. The missionary's wife needs to be able to meet some ladies on the street and learn to communicate with them. She needs to invite them over for tea and treat them to some American pastries and chat. However, American missionaries have been taught to live on compounds where they can eat American food, wear American clothes, watch American television and talk to each other in the American language. Compounds can almost make it seem as if they are not living in a foreign country. I believe this way of life on the mission field is especially damaging for the wives, who are abandoned to becoming housewives of the compound rather than functioning, productive "missionaries."

My recommendation to all missionary families is to get off

of the compounds and live in the communities. Assign every missionary to live in a different neighborhood. His assignment is to get to know every single family on his street. I mean he should know the first and last name of each family member, their ages, each one's birthday, where the adult family members work, where the children go to school, and any other pertinent information. Attend their graduation ceremonies, go to their promotional ceremonies, or be a visitor on a special day at their school. Buy your groceries from their little stand or from their little shop at their house. Do what you can to get to know them and to become a part of their community. Show them that you want to be one of them—not just be that unnamed, unknown missionary from America who lives in the middle of the block. You can still help out the senior missionary at his church on Sunday, but you could also start a Bible study at your home for your neighborhood where everybody knows you. In short order, you will have a church of your own. Congratulations! You're a missionary now.

This concept of segregation from the citizens can even extend into the ministry and fellowship. In the early years of our ministry, I spent a lot of time in Thailand because that is where the Final Frontiers outreach began. Sometime around 1990, I was invited by a missionary friend to an evening fellowship with his family. I learned that every Sunday night the missionaries around Bangkok would meet together for fellowship. It was a time for them to speak English, conduct a Bible study, watch a baseball game, host a cookout, and just to let their hair down and be American. I thought it was peculiar that they had this fellowship on Sunday nights, but I quickly learned that none of them had a Sunday night service at their church. Of course, that is not a sin, but I had to wonder if their supporting churches were aware of the nonexistent Sunday evening services so that their missionaries could have this time of fellowship.

That night I was asked a lot of questions because missionaries are by nature a curious people, and they want to know about God's work all over the world. Before the fellowship ended, the group had extended a call for me to move to Bangkok and to start a church—not for the Thai people—but for them! They asked me to be their pastor. Because mine is a peculiar calling that would preclude the possibility of such a position, I immediately turned them down without even considering it. Besides, my pastoring days were over. I felt I had long since served my time as a pastor, and whatever the sins of my youth were that led to such punishment, they surely were by then absolved!

As I spent time with God's servants around the world, it became apparent that there was a real loneliness in their hearts. Though they were happy to be where they were, there was a bitter nagging that accosted them, not so much to long for home, but to get away from those who surrounded them day after day, year after year.

On another trip to Thailand, I had been in the North working among some tribal groups. I have never just taken a vacation abroad or even taken a few days to relax. In most cases, I don't even go to the tourist sites. I'm not against it; I just don't have time for it. On this particular occasion, our national director needed to take a trip down the peninsula of Thailand. Since I had never been there, I asked if I could come along. I was excited to do so because it meant the opportunity for a train ride, which for some reason I really love.

We made our way south for a few hours and finally arrived in the coastal city of Hua Hin, located on the Gulf of Thailand. Pastor Kiatisak, our director, suggested that we go to a certain guest house that was known to be owned by Christians. In fact, it had been founded by a missionary couple from either England or Australia, I don't remember which. By this time the husband had died, and the elderly wife was the sole proprietor. When we arrived at the facility, I noticed that it was an older, but well-maintained Thai-style house located on the beach. Upon walking out on the sandy beach, I looked to the north and could see the outline of the downtown area maybe two miles away. It was quiet and serene. I was exhausted from living in the tribal villages for the past few weeks and existing on sticky rice, bamboo worms, and dogs, so a bed with a fan and a prepared meal was all I could think about. After walking around the property and not being approached by anyone, we made our way into the house to look for the manager and secure a room. We were asked to take a seat, and before long we were served cold water and received a visit from the missionary/owner. She was curious about us and had many unusual questions.

After a short period, I noticed guests walking past us to go to the dining room. We had a fair share of curious stares coming our way, but that is not uncommon. The lady explained that I could get a room for a certain amount, and that amount included three meals a day. In fact, the guests were congregating for lunch even as we spoke. I told her that the price was satisfactory, that we would like to book a room for two days, and that we would need a second bed for our room so that Kiatisak and I would not have to share a bed. It was at that moment that I must have slipped into a coma...

No sooner had the words left my mouth than she interrupted me and emphatically told me that I was welcome to stay but that the Thai pastor could not. She explained, "The missionaries who come here need to have a place to rest and relax away from the Thai people. You just can't be around them all the time without going a little crazy. We don't allow any Thai except for the cleaning staff in our facility. No Thai has ever slept in any of our beds. Even our food is Western style."

I looked at her and tried to retain the Southern-gentleman upbringing my mother had given me, but it was difficult. I asked her bluntly, "Are you aware that we are in Thailand, and it is filled with Thai people?"

"Oh, yes," she replied with a hint of disgust, "but none of them stay here."

About that time we arrived at the dining table since we had

been walking and talking for the past few moments. She asked if I would like to have lunch with them. I looked at her and then at the guests who by now were either in as much shock as I was or else in fear that my Thai pastor friend might actually attempt to sit down beside them. I told her as politely as I could that I thought it would be better if we looked for a meal somewhere else, and we left.

I must admit that I was angry. The thought of having a guest house for God's workers and excluding the Thai was outrageous to me then, and it still is today. But equally outrageous is the idea that a family was being supported as "missionaries" by dozens of American churches who thought they were actually witnessing, helping, and (God forbid) loving the Thai people. Instead, they were fostering a guest house of bigotry and racism in the guise of serving God.

Since that day, Kiatisak and I have often joked about taking a vacation in Hua Hin. I don't know whether or not we could stay there now because the missionary left Thailand two years later and sold her ministry/guest house/business. I always joked with Kiatisak saying, "I wish I could buy it; I would turn it into a vacation place for Thai pastors and Thai Christians and not let any foreigners stay there!" (Except myself, of course!)

The "Rookie-Assignments-Vs.-Church-Planting" Mind-set

Another word of advice to the veteran missionaries is to eliminate these "rookie assignments" that are given to the newcomers and which monopolize their time and keep them from church planting. I have had missionaries tell me that when they got to the mission field, their board told them that their job was to live at a camp facility owned by the mission board and to cut the grass and be the maintenance man. Of course, a missionary worth his salt will say, "I didn't come here to cut grass. I came here to plant churches."

I am not saying that a person shouldn't be willing to do whatever he needs to do; all I am saying is that he should make sure he does what God called him there to do. I am not opposed to a rookie missionary being submissive, loyal, and humble, but I am opposed to taking it to an illogical conclusion. God called him there as a missionary to plant churches. The churches supporting him are supporting him to plant churches, so if he is doing nothing more than cutting the grass, then he should send back his support money because the churches thought they were supporting a missionary.

Around 1993 I met with one missionary in the Caribbean who was complaining because I wanted to support national preachers on the island. All he did was complain the several days I was there. He complained because one of the missionaries who had retired and left had given his old car to one of the national preachers. He ridiculed and mocked the fellow within earshot, saying as he spoke to me, "Why did he give that guy a car! He doesn't even know how to change the oil!" In other words, it's ridiculous to give a national preacher a car when he doesn't even have enough experience with the car to know that he needs to change the oil or know how to change the oil.

My immediate response to him was muted because his wife was standing next to him, and I did not want to humiliate him. (Yes, I can be nice when I really try hard—sometimes.) So, I simply responded, "Maybe you could teach him how to change the oil." He grumbled some reply and walked away.

The American people have a crazy idea of missions as being anything but church planting. (Just today I heard a radio announcement of an upcoming mission conference in an Augusta area church. The announcer summarized missionaries as "whether teaching English, working at a university, or pastoring a church." No mention was made of church planting.)

That same missionary, when I discussed his job with him, told me that his function was to teach Sunday school at the church he attends and to teach computer classes at the Bible college on that property. I thought that was rather interesting because not everybody had a computer in 1993. I then asked him, "How many students do you have?"

And he replied, "Three."

"Do they have computers?" I asked.

When he answered, "No," I asked, "Well, how do you teach them computers if they don't have computers?"

He said, "We have a computer at the school, and I teach them on that."

"But, they don't have a computer that they can use when they go home?"

When he answered, "No," I asked, "Well then, what good does it do to teach them how to work with computers if they don't have a computer to use? Can they use the one at school?"

He replied, "No, they are not allowed to come to the school and use it personally; it's just there for their classes."

Can you see how utterly stupid and ridiculous that entire conversation was? Does it begin to help you understand why I may come across a little strong in my support for national church planters and disdain for lazy, dishonest men who call themselves missionaries?

But here's something even more ridiculous. When I asked him, "What else do you do?"—that was it. All he did was teach a Sunday school class and teach a computer class. Trying to salvage his dignity, I asked, "How many hours a week do you teach computer classes?"

He responded, "Three."

So this "missionary" teaches computer three hours a week to national preachers who don't have computers of their own at home to use and who are not allowed to use the school's computer, and he teaches a Sunday school class. Let's say he studies for an hour for that class, and it takes him an hour to teach it. So he's actually involved in ministry maybe five hours a week, but he is receiving full support as a missionary. This man at that time was probably 60 years old, so he had been on the mission field for a good 30 to 35 years, and by his own admission, he taught a Sunday school class and a computer class. How truly sad it was that he was not in the least ashamed of his answers, but he was vehemently opposed to my supporting these church planters because to do so would, in his estimation, "ruin" them.

How many of his supporting churches do you think knew that was the extent of his ministry? I can guarantee that 100 percent of his supporting churches thought that he was out knocking on doors or teaching Bible classes at their college there and planting churches. How many of these churches would have supported this man if they knew he was working five hours a week? Right—none! This conversation kind of makes you wonder what his reports to his supporting churches talked about, doesn't it?

Some Attitudes That Destroy Partnership With the National Pastors and Leaders

Another avenue to consider about these mind-sets that cause missionaries to become unproductive once they get to the mission field is the need for veteran missionaries to teach the novices about the attitudes and actions that can destroy partnerships with the nationals. To what am I referring? Some of the predominant destructive attitudes include pride, accentuating one's affluence, stating one's opinion without invitation, trying to control the ministries of the nationals, laziness, misrepresentation of the nationals work as their works, ignorance of the nationals' ways and culture, and personal cultural repulsions. Allow me to expound on those I have listed.

❖

The Mind-set of Pride

I know a lot about pride from personal experience. Whether or not the American people realize it, they are taught that they are the hope of the world. Many missionaries get off the plane with the feeling in their heart that now that they have arrived, "their" country will finally hear the Gospel. They totally dis-

count the fact that there have been missionaries before them—
maybe for as long a period of time as a hundred years. They totally discount the fact that national preachers struggle to
faithfully preach the Word of God in spite of their abject
poverty. American missionaries have the feeling that since they
have arrived, the job will *finally* get done.

Some missionaries compound the insult by writing home
that they plan to start a church in a certain town because there
are "no Gospel-preaching churches there." What they really
mean is that there are no churches there started by another
missionary from their own board. There may be Bible-preaching
churches there, but they are all relegated to not being a "Bible-
preaching church" merely because the "new kid on the block"
has not yet started his work. How prideful and absurd! They
have insulted not only the sacrifice of the missionaries already
there, but also the churches started and pastored by the national pastors.

As a footnote, let me add that Final Frontiers also experiences this from time to time. Another organization that uses
the same methods and philosophy as Final Frontiers often goes
to other countries to find pockets of preachers to support.
Rather than look for their own preachers to support, they tend
to seek out the groups with whom we work, promise them the
moon, and then tell them that Jon Nelms and Final Frontiers
are not Baptists and try to steal our workers. Their logic is that
since the term "Baptist" is not part of our name, we are not
Baptists. Using their own logic, since they don't have the word
"Christian" in their name, they must not be Christians.

If the attitude of pride is visible on their face, in their voice,
and in their actions, it makes them ineffective missionaries.

❖❖

The Mind-set of Affluence

There is nothing wrong with being wealthy. I wish every missionary had access to a bank account like the one Bill Gates
has—myself included. I really do. There is not a problem in the

world with being wealthy. Some of our greatest heroes of the faith were blessed abundantly by God. Abraham, Job, and many of the kings like David and Solomon were incredibly wealthy; some were wealthy beyond comprehension. Joseph of Arimathaea was one of the wealthiest men in the world in his day.

Nothing is wrong with being wealthy, but striving to be wealthy instead of striving to be Godly is wrong. A Christian who emphasizes working to make money instead of working to produce salvation decisions and planting churches has the wrong values. When a Christian's life is driven by money rather than by ministry, it is a problem. Many missionaries fall into this trap.

They start just as I once did, trying to make money to help subsidize the ministry. Because of having no experience in the business world, it takes more and more time away from ministry because the missionary now has to run his business. He has to take care of his employees, attend meetings, and conduct interviews. The next thing he knows, he is on this foreign field as a businessman—not a missionary.

It would be far better to partner with a businessman like the Apostle Paul partnered with the physician Luke and let the businessman support the ministry while the missionary does the ministry. Not only would that help the missionary, but it would also get more Christians on the field serving God rather than just warming the pews in American churches.

❖

The Mind-set of Control

My definition of control is a missionary's attempt to tell the nationals how to run their churches and the order of services, which really are cultural issues. American missionaries tend to think they know it all because they are college trained, have sufficient money available to pay for what they want, and possess the wherewithal to have things done the way they want. A missionary with control issues might be successful in getting the hirelings to work under those conditions, but no self-respecting man of God will.

Unfortunately, the idea of "control" is one of the most damaging philosophies of missions that has ever been created and perpetuated. It is common for instructors and boards to instill in the missionary candidates the idea that their success (generally measured by numbers) is dependent on the strength of their control over "the natives." Future missionaries are taught to keep the nationals at arm's length, to avoid fellowship outside of the church or visitation, and to maintain a lifestyle of separation from these good people.

Within the first decade of Final Frontiers, as I would travel from country to country meeting and consulting with missionaries, I began to see some patterns emerging. Some missionaries obeyed their boards and emulated the controllers who had come before them. Other missionaries, as far as their board was concerned, were ruling by the party lines, so to speak. However, privately, they often shared ministry and meals with the national pastors. Such deviation from the prescribed method of maintaining control would not remain covert for long, and many were fired from their boards or voluntarily quit their boards before they were terminated. The downfall they all shared in common was their friendship and partnership with the national leaders.

One missionary in South America who was from a famous, fundamental, independent Baptist board told me that he was reprimanded by the senior missionary in the country where he was serving because he frequently invited the national pastors to his home for a meal and fellowship. He was warned that such behavior would not be tolerated. When asked why it was a problem, the missionary was told that if he became "friends" with the national pastors, he would ultimately "lose control over them." Shocked by such a statement (as I am sure you who read this are), he then asked, "Then what am I to do when we are out doing visitation and it comes time to eat lunch?"

To his dismay, the answer given was, "You go inside the restaurant to eat and let him eat on the street."

This missionary quickly became one of the army of men around the world who have chosen to break fellowship with their board rather than with their national partners. I salute them. A major problem for such missionaries is that their boards have a copy of their mailing list. Out of due diligence, the board must then write to inform all of the missionary's supporting churches that he is no longer serving with them. This letter can easily carry the connotation that he was not submissive to their authority. In any case, such a letter gives a sense of comfort and convenience to some of the supporting pastors whose missions budgets are almost always critically low. They have been handed a justifiable excuse, in their minds, to drop this man's support, and they often do so without even contacting or consulting the missionary to hear his point of view.

The Mind-set of Laziness

A missionary's being called lazy is not always deserved, but it seems that one apple, though he may not be able to spoil the whole barrel, certainly can make everyone who looks into the barrel not want to eat from it. Ask a group of national preachers who really adore a missionary why they adore him, and I guarantee you they will say, "He eats our food, sleeps in our houses, and he works himself to death beside us. He loves us." But ask them to talk about other missionaries with whom they seem to have little contact, and they will report, "That guy is lazy. We only see him on Sunday. He drives his Land Rover to our church to teach a Sunday school class; when Sunday school is over he leaves. Sometimes he doesn't even stay for the service. We don't know what he does during the week. He said he's preparing Bible studies, but he doesn't teach them here. He says he's providing a teaching curriculum, but he's not discipling anyone."

Oftentime missionaries get the reputation of being lazy because they are lazy. Nobody makes a missionary punch a clock. Nobody stands behind a missionary looking over his shoulder.

The good churches sending support praise their missionaries for every little thing they do, as if it's something magnificent. They could pile up a mole hill, and they would call it a mountain. Over time, some missionaries even start believing how great they are! But the nationals know better, and so do the other missionaries who serve there. The highest expectation most supporting churches give to a missionary is that he "go" and give little concern to what he does once he gets there.

❖

The "Misrepresenting-the-Work-of-the-Nationals-as-Theirs" Mind-set

Of all the mistakes made by missionaries, this one really gets to me and to the national pastors. I don't know how many times, all around the world, I have had national workers and preachers complain about this misrepresentation to me. "A certain missionary came to our church and took pictures, asked me if I had any pictures he could use, and I gave him some. Then he went back to America on his furlough and used the pictures of our work to raise support for his family and didn't give us anything—not even an offering."

That's wrong! When a missionary needs to raise support, he should show what he has been doing—not what somebody else has been doing! When borrowing a picture for a video presentation, the missionary must make sure he "gives credit to whom credit is due." He should acknowledge that the photo was given to him by Missionary So-and-So or National Preacher So-and-So and that he is showing it to illustrate a point. He should not take the credit for another man's work.

I once saw a missionary presentation and heard the missionary, whom I knew as a friend, imply that the church in which he was seen preaching was a church he had started and that he had led the interpreter, who happens to be the pastor, to Christ. I knew for a fact that the photo was one of a series taken from a week-long revival where different missionaries were invited to come speak at this church which had been started by a national preacher. That pastor/interpreter was saved and pastoring while this missionary was still a teenager in Bible college in the United States! What dishonesty! But his dishonesty did not stop him from receiving a big love offering and monthly support.

❖

The Mind-set of Ignorance

Many missionaries go to the field with the attitude that they know it all, not realizing how ignorant they really are. That ignorance shines brightly. Some missionaries become a joke to the nationals, but only a joke they tell when missionary is not paying attention or until he learns their language. The nationals make jokes because of the silly things that missionaries do or the funny way they say things or the mistakes that they make. Generally, the nationals do not mind if missionaries make verbal mistakes; they love to laugh at an American's mispronunciations and grammatical errors in their language.

What the nationals have a difficult time understanding is the missionary's pride that rejects their grammatical corrections or the little insults about their countrymen, culture, or situation. There are times when Americans tend to go overboard. Nobody really wants to eat with dirty hands or to eat from a filthy plate. It has become common to see Americans carrying around squeeze bottles of antibacterial gel. It is probably wise to use one, but some of them go so crazy about it—to the point of insulting the people to whom they are ministering. I think some husbands wouldn't kiss their wife unless she gargled with a bottle of antibacterial gel first.

❖

The Mind-set of Cultural Repulsion
Meaning "Ours, Not Theirs"

This ignorance leads to what could be referred to as "cultural repulsion." If the foreigner's ignorance catches the nationals' attention, it is because that display of ignorance is repugnant to them. Let me explain.

Several years ago I was in India with my wife and several other guests, including my pastor, Don Prosser. These folks, who were troopers, never complained about the heat, the pollution, the food—nothing. One afternoon we attended a church dedication. My friends and former missionaries to Thailand, Vietnam, and Sri Lanka, Tim and Vanessa Ekno, met one of the national directors that had already built several church buildings for the leper congregations in Andhra Pradesh.

During this day, we had taken a rather dusty, dirty ride to the church in an open-windowed van. We were covered with dust, dirt, and grime. After arriving, we had shaken the hands of many people, including more than a hundred lepers who were not accustomed to soap. Then we had provided food for them because it was an inauguration service. They were sitting on the floor to eat, so we had to constantly bend over to serve them. More than once, most of us had placed our palms on the dirty floor to keep from falling over when we bent down. (For me, it's a fat man vs. gravity thing!) Now it was time for us to eat. We sat at the table, and they served us.

Immediately, someone picked up a bottle of antibacterial gel and handed it to me. Believing everyone else was as dirty as I was, I began to offer it to each of the guests with me. Maybe ten seconds later our national director, Pastor Swatantra Kumar came to me and politely (but firmly) said, "You should not use that to clean your hands. You are insulting the people. It makes them think that they are dirty, and you have to clean yourself after touching them." We stopped using the gel immediately.

I should have known better. It was not my intention to insult anyone, and Pastor Kumar knows that I love the lepers. I hug them, hold them, and adore them, but my very action of innocently and logically wanting to clean my hands suggested that I was superior to them and needed to be clean after touching them. I was ashamed that, with all my cultural knowledge and experience, I had not discerned the situation more wisely. I was sorry that I had put my host in a position to have to correct me—his partner and his benefactor. But I was so proud that he cared more for the poor lepers' feelings than he did for mine, even though I am the one who finances his entire ministry and supports nearly 200 of his preachers.

When I first started going to Thailand as a missionary, I made so many mistakes in ignorance. All over Thailand, but particularly in the Bangkok area which is at sea level or below, each household has a threshold at the front door that is about five inches high. The threshold is to keep floodwater out when it rains.

The Thai are Buddhists, but they are also animists. The people believe that demon spirits occupy every piece of land, so erecting a building on any piece of property will disrupt the spirit's home. Therefore, the property owners must build a spirit house on that property. To fail in doing this will bring insult to the spirit, and that spirit will retaliate with sickness, death, loss of income, or any other kind of misfortune. The spirit houses look like very ornate bird houses that are decorated with flowers and greenery. The people put miniature images of birds or people or gods or spirits inside the spirit house with the belief that the spirits occupy those images. The owners of the spirit houses provide their spirits with bananas, grapes, and even miniature glasses of water, so that they won't bother them or their family.

Some people also believe that some of these spirits actually live in the threshold. For that reason a Thai person entering his home never steps on the threshold. If their sandals are dirty, they don't scrape them off on the threshold like Americans often do. Instead, they take off their shoes and leave them outside. This is not just Thai culture; nearly all Asians do the same. Why? Because they know what they've been stepping in all day long and they don't want to track that into their home where their babies are playing on the floor. They want their home to be clean and sanitary.

This is just one reason why the Asians look upon Americans

as barbarians. How ironic that Americans think foreigners are the barbarians, and foreigners think Americans are! I think in this case they're right! Think about it. In what do you step in public bathrooms, in the lawn where the dog plays, as well as all the other places you go? Then you walk inside your house and transfer this filth and germs to the carpet, or more accurately, between the threads of the carpet. Then you put your babies down to play on that dirty carpet. What are they rolling around in? You see, Americans are barbarians!

So in Asia you always take your shoes off before you go into a home, and you never step on the threshold. Something else you never do in Thailand is point your foot at another person. A man's crossing his legs and pointing the bottom of his shoes at someone else in the room is a no-no in Asia. You never touch anyone on their head because their head is a sacred place, and it's not to be touched.

What did I do as an inexperienced missionary? When I was out visiting the slums, literally walking through sewer water and everything else from dirt, mud, filth, trash, to dead rats, I stopped to visit at a certain home, and I was invited in. I looked down at my feet before entering the home and noticed the filth all over my shoes. I quickly scraped off my shoes on the threshold of their doorway and then stepped inside after getting off as much as possible, but I still tracked dirt and filth inside their home. I then sat down and crossed my legs out of habit, and my muddy, filthy shoes were pointed at one of their family members.

I had just made an obscene gesture in their culture that has no equal in ours. The pointing of the middle finger at someone in the American culture does not begin to compare to what a person's pointing the bottom of his foot is in Asia.

So there I sat pointing my dirty shoe at someone. When their child walked in the door, I stood up, brushed my fingers through his hair, and said, "What a cute little boy you have." When I sat back down and began to tell these people about my

God Who gave His life for them, in the immortal words of Gomer Pyle, USMC, "Surprise! Surprise! Surprise!" they were not interested. I thought to myself, "These people are hardhearted, or I don't know the language as well as I thought I did."

No, the problem is I did everything I could do, but from a cultural standpoint, I did it wrong because of my ignorance. For that reason, the very people I was trying to reach didn't want to have anything to do with my God. But if a veteran missionary had simply explained to me what to do and what not to do, an event like that could have been avoided.

From that time on since early 1987, any time I go to visit a country, especially for the first time, I tell the national director when he picks me up at the airport to "consider me like a dry sponge who wants to soak up the culture while I'm there. I want to do it correctly, so if I do anything or say anything that's incorrect, please tell me. I promise that I will not be offended and my feelings won't be hurt. I just want to know so that I don't make mistakes."

A big smile always comes across my host's face, and he is thankful to have someone visiting with that humility and willingness to learn. They all oblige me, as Pastor Kumar did by instructing, "You did this wrong. You said that wrong. Don't do it that way; do it this way." The result is that you learn, and that is what is so important.

One of the main problems on the mission field is that a missionary often has an improper mind-set or a mind-set that keeps him doing the wrong thing over and over again. The American way may well be the best way—but only if you are in America. Likewise, their way is the best way—when you are in their land.

Most of what I have described as the attitudes that kill relationships with the national church leaders can be summarized in the following illustration that is, unfortunately, true.

In the mid-1990s, I was invited to travel to the Philippines to speak at an international conference on fundamentalism.

These conferences occur from time to time and are financed and arranged by a certain camp of fundamentalism which is represented by a fair number of good churches made up of good members. Those whom I have known personally over the years are fine folks who have no idea of the behind-the-scenes politics that go on.

This particular conference was being organized by a good Christian doctor from Singapore whom I had met years earlier in northern Thailand. He had gone there often with a team of doctors to treat the tribal people and had helped to evangelize them through the medium of medicine. Over the years he had heard of Final Frontiers and had made arrangements to first call and then meet me. He was a gracious man who actually contributed a very large check to our ministry when we were building our current office facility in 1995. (Incidentally, he never referred to himself as a "missionary doctor"; he was just a doctor who went out and did missionary work and medical ministry.) Though he did not support the Thai tribal preachers, this brother did have a heart for them and often donated funds to build churches and hostels for the children.

I think since Final Frontiers does not concentrate on building and since he did not concentrate on support, he felt we were a good match. At one point I even invited his team to India to participate in one of our crusades by treating the sick who came to our services.

After seeing the work that our preachers were able to accomplish with subsidies from Final Frontiers, he asked me to come to the Philippines to speak at a national pastors' gathering. He was tasked with the organization and selection of speakers, though the host was actually from a certain Bible college in the United States.

Several months before the conference, I visited my doctor friend in Singapore as he desired for us to spend some time together. While there I had a good time and met some of his pastor friends who were kind, but I couldn't help but notice they

182 ❖ The Great Omission

had some strange practices such as baptizing babies, even though they considered themselves to be "baptistic fundamentalists." Of course, none of these men were seeking support as they were all very well-paid pastors, so their particular doctrinal differences, though strange and defended more as a custom than doctrine, were of very little personal concern to me.

Before the convention, I was asked to submit an outline of my lecture, which I gladly fulfilled. I had been asked to come and speak to the men about being supported by churches in the United States and to encourage them to have an evangelistic zeal for winning their own people. To this day I still have the outline that was returned to me by both the coordinator and the American missionary that has written on it, "Great, this is exactly what we need." In fact the coordinator told me that I was the only speaker who did provide an outline as he had requested.

When the time for the conference arrived, I was met by my friend at the Manila airport and taken to my lodgings at a nice hotel in town, just blocks from the convention center. I had arranged for our Thai national director, Rev. Kiatisak Siripanadorn, to accompany me, as well as our Indian national director, Pastor K. S. Kumar and his wife. I immediately began to notice that not only were both of these men being treated with contempt and condescension by the other American speakers (pastors, missionaries and professors), but that I too was being kept at arm's length.

On the first day of the three-day conference, I studied the schedule and noticed that all the segments were set at 45 minutes except for the one immediately preceding mine, which was a seminar on church music. That seminar had been allotted a total of nine hours—three hours each day. I thought it strange that in a foreign land, the "experts" from America were coming to teach rather than to learn and that four times as much time was given for musical instruction than for any other subject. I would have found this schedule strange if the meeting was being held in Miami, but I found it all the more strange being in Manila where the Philippine people have their own cultural musical tastes and styles. I had thought the speakers were there to help, encourage, and motivate the national people— not to remake their song services into an image straight from America.

When I began to speak, I naturally had the attention of all the preachers since I was speaking about support. I did suggest that they not come to the United States to raise support; rather, I suggested they remain in their land and let Final Frontiers or some other ministry raise support for them. I have always felt it to be ridiculous to bring national preachers to America to raise their support for many reasons including the following:

(1) They tend to stay in America and never leave.

(2) They go home with as much money as an American missionary raises and really, why shouldn't they? The problem is the other national preachers begin to look upon them as greedy opportunists and feel they have "national" skin but an American mind and heart.

I thought the service went well. That evening I did something I had never done before and have never done since. I told all the missionary wives in the nursery that I would watch the children for them so they could attend the services. What an experience! Later it was reported that I was unfriendly and did not even speak to any missionary while at the conference. I had, according to the report, come to sow discord. In their emails that "found their way" to me in the following months, I was accused of being the "anti-Christ" and being "Satan's number-one tool for the destruction of the modern-day missions movement."

"What has brought on all this condemnation?" I wondered.

The next morning of the conference, I had gone to the hotel restaurant to have breakfast. I noticed Pastor Kumar and his wife, so I sat with them to enjoy the fellowship. A few minutes later, the coordinator came and asked if he could sit with us. Of course we were glad to break bread with him. No sooner did he take his seat, than he began to tell me that I was corrupting the hearts of the Filipino pastors by causing them to think about money rather than ministry.

Now you must know that I can feign humility with the best of them, and I always prefer calmness to confrontation. So once accused, I asked what I had done. I don't remember his answer, but neither Pastor Kumar nor I could comprehend his conclusion from what he had said.

I pulled out the outline that I had used the day before and showed him that it was the original that I had sent to him on which he had written in his own hand, "This is exactly what we need." I asked how I could follow his approved and praiseworthy outline and, at the same time, be so destructive. The outline contained not only the points but also the illustrations that I would use.

Of course he had no answer to my question, but he continued to slay me with his venomous accusations. He also shared with me that none of the other preachers on the team liked me or wanted to be around me. (That point was reinforced 30 minutes later when the vans pulled up to take us to the convention center. One was full already, and the other had three men inside. When I entered and sat on the back seat of the van, the three men got out and crowded into the already full van. I had a very comfortable ride to the convention center.)

After hearing the accusations and while still sitting at the table, I tried to change the subject and began to ask him questions. The conversation went something like this. I'll call him "Brother Bob," though I don't remember his real name.

"Well, Brother Bob, thank you for your opinion and correction. I know you mean well and want only the best for these men. Perhaps if I had been here as long as you, I would have a better grip on the culture and know what to say and how to say it. How long have you been here by the way?"

To my question he replied, "Seventeen years."

"Wow," I said, "seventeen years. I had no idea. I guess by now you must have the language totally mastered."

Surprisingly, he replied, "No, I don't speak the local languages. I only speak English."

Pastor Kumar looked at me as if he couldn't decide whether to laugh or cry. I felt bad for the missionary, so I remarked, "Oh, well, you live in Manila, and since so many people here speak English, it probably doesn't matter." Trying to change the subject and save face for him, I asked, "How many churches have you started here?"

He looked at me as if I had an agenda and responded, "None, I administrate a Bible college that I started." Once again, my attempt to save face for him fell flat, so I pivoted to set him up for a compliment by saying, "Oh, that's great! How many students do you have?" In a brief moment he slapped away the life preserver I was trying to hand him by replying simply, "Three."

I was desperately trying to dance my way out of this pit that I was unintentionally digging, but my feet were stuck to the floor. In a final attempt to end on this subject and hope to find a new one to pursue, I asked him the name of his school.

He replied, "The ___ ___ Memorial Bible College." (Insert in the blanks the name of any long-deceased fundamentalist preacher known for strict, conservative standards, but one who is virtually unknown to the Filipino churches.) I don't want to share the actual name of this man's hero because others of his followers would consider that to be a criticism, though it really would be just stating the fact of his name. Besides, I have enough enemies already.

After three days we moved to a large church in Mindanao, and the speakers who had been there came to Manila. Once we arrived, I was taken aside and was told that I would not be able to speak anymore. For the rest of the time I was there, I just sat outside the facility. By that time I already knew everything I needed to know about church music anyway. I don't know how, but word of the tumult I was causing had reached Davao before me. The national pastors began to seek me out, skipping their altered seminars in order to speak with me. From that day on, I took all my meals with the nationals—not just out of necessity, but also out of choice.

A myriad of other events occurred during that week, but I think I have sufficiently provided a glimpse of how my ministry and philosophy was accepted in the early days. Those who have followed Final Frontiers and imitated our work travel on a philosophical and Biblical path that was paved with many tears, trials, and rejections. They have no idea. These feelings and attitudes of superiority over the national preachers cause these good men to reject partnership with the missionaries. This particular conference has never again been held in the Philippines, nor was it welcomed because of the condescending attitude of the organizers and the other speakers. I have been in the Philippines many times and maintain a ministry there nearly two decades later. To God be the glory!

The "They-Don't-Speak-Spanish-in-Mexico" Mind-set

As I have previously mentioned, many countries are occupied by ethnic groups that do not speak the native or national language. It has been said that over 1,700 languages and dialects exist in India alone. Most of these have a common root, but others are as foreign as Russian is to English.

Individual languages come from one of 128 language families, and these language families come from language roots. At the time of the Tower of Babel, Bible scholars estimated that 70 languages had been created by God. By the time of Christ, those 70 languages had multiplied to some 60,000 separate languages. Since the time of Christ, due to conquests and assimilation, extinction and annihilation, only some 24,000 languages still remain. About half of the people representing these 24,000 languages have had exposure to the Gospel; the other half have not.

In my travels, it is common to pick up enough words to be able to get by. Years ago when I moved to Honduras, I hired a young lady to teach me Spanish. My intention was to hire someone who could not speak English so that I would not use it as a crutch. I hired this lady to be an assistant to my family, helping us shop, learn the taxi routes, etc. As a result, I learned to speak Spanish like a toddler. Mine was a natural acquisition of the language, and to this day, I have never had a single lesson in Spanish. Of course, I am not a perfectly fluent speaker, and the longer I am away from the Latin world, the fewer words I remember. Even while there, I was able to help establish several churches simply by using a translator.

What is interesting to me is that as I travel to other Latin countries, words often have a different meaning or do not even exist. Frankly, a person can get himself into a lot of trouble in traveling from country to country as what may be a common noun in one country is a verb of derision in another. Assuming words have the same meaning can be embarrassing to say the least.

But that is not really what I am addressing. In some countries, the indigenous population refuses to speak the national language. They see it as the language of their conquerors and refuse to submit to it. Throughout history, it has been common for the conqueror to abolish the native tongue in an attempt to destroy the unity and nationalistic pride of the people. This practice was especially true in recent decades during the expansion of Communism around the globe. Before then, language banning was commonly, if not universally, practiced by the Spaniards in the "New World," and before them, the Muslims, Romans, Chaldeans, and Egyptians (among others) banned indigenous languages.

The point is that just because a person is in Mexico does not mean the people understand him when he speaks Spanish. The people with whom he is attempting to communicate may speak one of the 68 languages of the indigenous Indians spoken there. At best, Spanish is their second language. In fact, while many are bilingual, 5.4 percent of the population does not speak Spanish at all. That is over half of the native Indian population living in Mexico, representing 6,073,318 souls. Included in these statistics are 15 languages with more than 100,000 speakers and 34 languages with less than 20,000 speakers. Typically, the smaller the people group (or ethnos), the less likely they will ever be exposed to the Gospel. While "they may all look alike to us," they are as different from each other as they are from me. Surprisingly, there are 52 countries whose populations are smaller than the number of "Mexicans" who don't speak Spanish. While many missionaries are called to those countries, few seem called to go to the non-Spanish-speaking "Mexicans."

The unfortunate reality is that there are missionaries on the field who could reach them, but they do not know they are there to be reached. Whoever provided their training did not tell these missionaries that just because people look Latino and just because they live in Mexico does not mean they speak Spanish.

Kenya, which is located on the east side of Africa, has a population of over 39 million people with 62 languages. Ghana, which is located in western Africa, has nearly 23 million people with 79 languages, plus multiplied dialects spoken by various indigenous tribes. China has 1,312,979,000 people. Nine percent of the people, which computes to over 123 million, are minorities. Altogether, 296 languages are spoken in China, not counting the hundreds of dialects.

Frankly, one of the most discouraging facts about missions today, and for many decades, is that missionaries are not being taught the importance of learning who is living in the country where they have chosen to minister. They have no concept of demographics, whether it be of the nation, the city, or even the street on which they reside. How can they effectively reach the people if they do not even know who is living there?

❖

The "Residency-Vs.-Tourist-or Work-Visas" Mind-set

Unfortunately, missionaries innocently do a myriad of things that hinder their ministry, and they do them only because that is the way these things have always been done. One of those pertains to their legal status in the foreign countries where they serve. Or better put, some missionaries with a tourist or missionary visa serve rather than live in the country they have chosen to serve with the status of "resident" or with a work visa. For some reason, missionaries have never been taught to obtain a residency in the countries where they serve. When foreigners come to the United Sates, the authorities want them to get a residency because it shows they want to be an American. They are not in the States just to use Americans, to take what Americans have and be gone. They want to mesh and merge with the American people.

Don't you know that the national people want to feel the same way about Americans when Americans go to their country? Nothing demonstrates that willingness to mesh and merge more than becoming a resident. When visitors make a short-term visit to America, they will obtain a tourist visa, which is usually limited to six months. If they are coming for a purpose, such as for education or employment, they will seek a student visa or a work visa or permit, which entitles them to have employment and pay taxes.

But if someone is literally moving his family and his belongings to America and leaving his own country, then that person must seek a permanent residency visa. To be here legally and live and work in America, one must have that permanent residency visa, which is more commonly known as a "green card." This green card entitles the person to all the privileges of this country with the exception of voting or holding public office. Otherwise, the person has the same rights that a citizen enjoys. This same status is available in probably every country of the world, and if not all, certainly the vast majority of them.

Unfortunately, because missionaries have not been taught to live in foreign countries in this manner, they are viewed as being "temporary" by the citizens who know that at the first hint of difficulty, such as a flood, hurricane, or civil unrest, those "temporary" residents will be at the airport with tickets in hand waiting for the first flight out. I am reminded of the words of I John 2:19 which says, *"They went out from us, but they were not of us; for if they had been of us, they would no doubt have continued with us: but they went out, that they might be made manifest that they were not all of us."* Though in context, this verse does not have that exact meaning, the words still remind me of this problem I see on the mission field.

A missionary who becomes a resident says to the people, "I want to be one of you. I am not here temporarily to do what I want to do and then can't wait to get out of here. I'm planning to live here the rest of my life." Some might wonder, "But what if you are not planning on living there the rest of your life?" If you are planning to be there for more than two or three years, then become a resident. To become a resident in most countries of the world will cost between $100 and $1,000. That's it. Becoming a resident will keep a missionary from having to fly in and out of that country every three to six months to fulfill his visa requirements.

I will address more about this subject later, but let me articulate the importance of becoming a resident. Being a resident means the missionary has rights in the country. He can work if times get tough, and he needs more income. It also means he can legally receive a salary from his church or ministry.

I understand that there are those who say missionaries cannot work in a foreign country. That is a true statement unless the missionary becomes a resident. A resident can easily obtain a work visa or a work permit in most cases. Then he can work, and the American churches will not have to keep sending support. Or they can send half of what they were sending and send the other half to national preachers in his country who are doing a bang-up job of evangelizing their own people. Or they can share the freed-up funds with another missionary who has a deficit.

❖

The Mind-set Toward Lifestyles

Finally, let me address the American style of living—his housing, his education, and so forth. Look, I was born American. I am an American culturally. But that does not mean that I have to flaunt my ways above other people. I am not one of those who believe that a missionary should live in a dump. I find it rather humorous that many times some pastors will complain about missionaries who live above their own people, but I know many a pastor who lives above the means of the average church members in his church. He drives a much nicer car, and he and his family live in a much nicer home.

Where is it written that an evangelist can drive a $100,000 motorhome and a pastor can drive a $60,000 Cadillac, but a missionary has to drive a broken-down dump? The logic is that missionaries should not live at a higher standard than the people to whom they minister, but the real reason is that the American people do not want to see their missionaries living at a standard higher than their own.

Let's face it, I have been in many churches where at Christmastime, the people will give their pastor a new Lincoln to drive. I have yet to see anybody give a missionary a Lincoln to drive. (And I wouldn't want one either—a utility vehicle maybe, but not a Lincoln!) So I think more care needs to be exercised when complaining about how missionaries live—especially when those complaining do the same.

Missionaries are people too. I want the best education I can get for my children. I want the best house I can get for my family to live in. But that does not mean I need to do it to the extent of turning off my witness to others. It just means I need to do the best I can do without going overboard, and in some countries, it doesn't take much to go overboard.

The point is that the missionary's home, no matter how poor or how wealthy, should always be open to their people. His home should not be a safe, secure area that the nationals aren't allowed to enter. It should be a welcome home to them as well. A missionary must realize that everything he has—no matter how poor or how fancy—belongs to God and is given to the missionary and his family for His purposes.

On the other hand, I have seen missionaries live to the opposite extreme. I am not opposed to a missionary's making that choice, and it may even impress the poorer people (though I am not really sure about that), but to the middle-class and higher, it makes them wonder about the mentality of a man who would choose to live in a dangerous slum when he could have his family living in a secure and clean environment. Of course, if the missionary's chosen field takes him to the jungle, such thoughts will never arise.

Some Mind-sets That Cause Missionaries to Quit

In addressing these particular mind-sets, I am addressing those who reached the field and seemingly made it. They learned from their mistakes. They learned what to do and what not to do. They jumped right in and got the job done, but then they quit. Statistics report that 55 percent of all missionaries who complete their first four-year term and return home for furlough never return to the field. Why? The number-one reason given is the "inability to adapt to the culture."

❖

The "It's-Not-Safe-to-Live-There" Mind-set

My family and I lived in Honduras in the latter part of the twentieth century. In October 1998 Hurricane Mitch slowly moved over the country of Honduras and literally stayed there for 30 days. The winds were not so devastating, but the amount of rain that fell on the country caused floods and mudslides countrywide. In some cases, entire villages were wiped out, and in those 30 days, more than 13,000 people lost their lives.

For more than a month, a shoot-on-sight curfew was enacted at 6:00 p.m. Virtually no one had water or other necessities. Because I had a car, I spent every day searching for food and water for my family and friends. Often I would see people on the side of the road wandering aimlessly.

One day I picked up a man in his thirties who was wearing nothing but an old pair of underwear. He had lived on one of the hillsides surrounding Tegucigalpa and had lost his family. He told me that a loud noise had awakened him from his sleep, so he went outside to see what it was. The noise he had heard was the crumbling houses as the water and mud destroyed everything in its path. He told me that he ran back inside his little two-room house to get his family, but as he did, the house began to slide out from under him. He wept as he told me that he had his wife's hand in his but could not hold onto her. Within a brief moment of time, he lost his father, his wife, and their two children, his house and all his possessions, except for the underwear he was wearing when I found him. I took the time to share the Gospel with him and give him food before taking him to the National University where the homeless were congregating.

For a month we had no water in our house. We would catch rain water in any container we could find. We could not flush the toilets and had to boil everything we drank. I knew the owner of a water delivery company and made arrangements to have water delivered to our home and to those of my friends, but the water truck could come at any time—even 2:00 a.m. When the driver honked the horn, we had to be ready for the delivery, or the truckers would move on to the next location.

Hurricane Mitch devastated the lives of the entire nation. Months later one of the Honduran people told me that the people respected us because we had stayed. At first I didn't understand what he meant by that statement. I thought, "Of course we stayed; this is where God has put us."

As we talked more, I began to understand what this man meant. Every missionary he knew had left the country as soon as news reports began forecasting Mitch's arrival. These missionaries who wanted to be out of danger demonstrated to the people of Honduras that they were not really part of them and did not want to be. They were fair-weather missionaries who would never be loved or accepted by the people.

My family and I did not stay because we felt we were better than other missionaries. We stayed because the idea of leaving never entered our minds. Why would anyone allow a natural event to drive them away from the place to which they claimed God had called them? While many missionaries were leaving, actors and politicians were coming in by the droves to see and to be seen. The unsaved came to serve while God's servants were retreating from the field of battle at the most opportune moment in the history of the nation. No, my family and I didn't stay because we made a conscientious decision to do so; we stayed because to do otherwise would have required a conscious decision to leave.

Acquiring a residency, which will cost anywhere from $100 to $2,000, says to the citizens that the missionary wants to be one of them and will be one with them. It endears him to the people, cements a bond that cannot be broken, and opens doors of ministry opportunities that are legion.

Let's say, for example, that in honor of his becoming a resident that a missionary has a party and invites everyone on his street to celebrate with him. I can guarantee that the people will be there. They want to sample that American chocolate cake and other foods and see how Americans celebrate. A celebratory party is a great opportunity for a missionary to get the nationals into his home and to tell them more about why he is there.

It will delight his church members to know that he is not just a missionary who will come and then leave at the first hint of disease or trouble. Most of the people in that foreign country would do anything to be able to move to and legally live in the United States; but to the contrary, this missionary has given up everything to be able to come and live with them. They can see that their missionary came not to gain wealth, not to lord over them, but to be their servant. How could a missionary possibly impress them more?

Tragedy is never a time to leave. When a tsunami hits, when bombs begin to drop, or when demonstrators are in the streets are all times when the missionary needs to "dig in"—for the long haul.

I can recall being in Esteli, Nicaragua, with my family for a 1992 crusade during the Communist takeover of the country. We didn't know it, but the little hotel where we were staying (if you want to call it a hotel; you can't call it a motel because in the Latin culture that word has an entirely different and derogatory meaning) was next door to a Sandinista ammunition warehouse, which was filled with hand grenades, mortars, tank shells, and everything else imaginable. All that separated us from the munitions warehouse was an adobe wall a few inches thick. Tanks rumbled down the street shooting off their guns in the middle of the night, and all that prevented the shrapnel from coming in our room was a five-inch mud wall and a tin roof over our heads.

To be honest, when we got back to our rooms, I went to bed and immediately fell asleep. My wife and kids fell so deeply asleep that people had to wake us up the next morning. We weren't afraid because the experiences we had already had gave us the assurance that God would take care of us. So why lose sleep over what was happening in the streets?

Sometimes the soldiers would line up a tank up at the end of a block and shoot a shell through every building in its path, killing as many as they could when the shell exploded. Cars and tires were burning, and people were lying dead in the street with blood splattered on the few walls still standing, yet there we were, passing out tracts.

At that time, we didn't even speak Spanish, but we were just doing our best to witness to people because that's why we were there. At night when the services would begin under the tent, at times we were surrounded by soldiers carrying machine guns. One night the military presence even shut down the services but allowed us to reopen the next day.

During the day, we would go up and down the main streets where people came to shop to give them a Gospel witness. A friend with me noticed that we were actually standing in front of the Sandinista party headquarters. I thought to myself, "Oh well, why not?" and we entered the building and began passing out tracts to the Communist leaders working there. After a few minutes, we were ushered upstairs. I thought we were about to be put in front of a firing squad or at least be tickled to death. Nervously, we entered the office of the Sandinista official who was the overseer of the northern Nicaragua region, a Sandinista hotspot. He took one of our tracts and studied it for a moment, then looked at us and asked, "Why didn't you come up here to give us some?"

We told him that we were working our way upstairs and would be glad for him to have one. In fact, we gave him several different tracts, and then he dismissed us. We went from office to office giving out a Gospel witness. As a result of our ministry that week, a church was planted that thrives today—nearly 20 years later.

A few months earlier we had been in the city of Ocotal, the home of a former prison that had been converted to a Sandinista interrogation center. (It is once again a prison.) In other words, those who were known to be or suspected to be Contras were taken there, "interrogated" for information, and then generally were never heard from again.

In the evenings we were holding services in a walled empty lot near the church we had there. There was not enough room in the church to hold the crowds, so the lot was used for overflow. The empty lot had an adobe wall around it—probably eight feet high. In the lot was a single tree. Each night as I preached, the limbs of the tree became seats for those who wanted a better view. I was reminded of the story of Zacchaeus, so I used that passage to present the Gospel, knowing that the people would be able to relate to it. Along the top of the wall sat men and children who also wanted a better view. As is the case in most third-world countries, when the wall was built and plastered, broken pieces of glass were embedded along the top to discourage burglars from climbing over. The people had smashed the pieces of broken glass and then placed thick blankets, folded cardboard, or other items to protect them from the remaining shards that they sat on.

One night during the invitation, a man came forward to accept Christ. I did not know this man. These were perilous times, and no one tried to bring attention to himself. Just a few months earlier a CIA plane carrying weapons and supplies to the Contras had been shot down nearby, and the pilot was captured. In Ocotal the event had been painted on a wall in the town, showing the American CIA pilot bound and wounded, being led to trial by a female Sandinista solder.

I looked inside that building, which served as a warehouse and saw that it was loaded with food supplies from Russia. Also inside were school books for the elementary school, which depicted scenes of Nicaraguan children armed with AK-47 assault rifles killing Americans. The brother of the dictator, Daniel Ortega, had publically announced that their soldiers would attack the United States and that the blood of Americans would flow in the streets.

As I have already mentioned, those were perilous times, and because of that, all missionaries had fled the country. To me, those perilous times presented an opportunity to reach those who were being forsaken and to care for the national preachers who needed food, Bibles, and encouragement. In my mind and in my heart, I believe that missionaries are or should be like firemen. Everyone knows that firemen do not run from fire: they run into it, looking for those whom they can rescue from the eternal flames.

As we preached night after night, we could see God doing a

marvelous work. Several weeks later I met the unknown man who had come forward to accept Christ. Hundreds had been saved, but this man was special. Unknown to me, he was a Sandinista officer who worked at that interrogation center. His job was to "interview" and then dispose of the people afterward. Because he had accepted Christ, he had resigned his commission and was going to the homes of those whom he had helped torture and then kill, asking for the remaining family members' forgiveness. To give the family closure, he told these grieving people what had happened and shared with them where the bodies were buried. He would then tell them why he wanted their forgiveness and that he had already received forgiveness from God. He used this hurt and heartache he had caused as a mighty witness throughout that region, and as a result, many came to Christ.

When I travel in the Middle East, I never know from one day to the next if I will be facing eternity. I have ridden in taxis in the Middle East where the people did not know we could speak the language, and the other people in the taxi/van were discussing how to give us to the terrorists or how to kidnap us and send us to Iraq to Abu Musab al Zarqawi so he can film us as he cuts off our heads.

I was sitting behind them listening to their plans to end my life, and they had no idea that I knew what they were planning. Do you really think I feel comfortable hearing that kind of talk or hearing somebody saying, "Let's take them to such-and-such place, and we'll shoot them"?

At times when I have been riding in taxis with my partners, we speak in English because the nationals cannot understand us, and we are making plans on how to escape from that taxi at the next stop! We make plans about which one of us will stay behind to hold off the driver and his companions while the others take off running! Of course, no one is ever willing to leave a brother behind, so the plans usually get scrapped, or we all just quickly jump out at the same time and disappear into the crowd.

Do I enjoy going to places like that? Well, yes, in some ways I do. I am one of those "weird" guys who enjoy the adrenaline rush. But I am aware of the fact that there is potential danger around every corner, that there are people who will walk up to an American on the street and spit in his face or even threaten, "I'm gonna cut your head off." They are bold because they are surrounded by their friends, and they think you don't know what they are saying to you. But we can be bold because we are under orders from our Commander to be there to do His bidding, and it is His responsibility to care for us—to whatever extent He chooses.

The "Hotdogs, Grasshoppers, and Mushrooms" Mind-set

As I have already written, I was on my first trip to Thailand when I found myself in an Akha village, later named Zion Hill. For dinner, the villagers served me among other edible items, hot "dogs," grasshoppers, and leeches. I thought the hot "dogs" were steak, and the leeches were just juicy mushrooms. It was obvious that the grasshoppers were really locusts. The food, except for the leeches, was good, and I even asked for seconds.

I am not the possessor of a weak stomach, but to be honest with you, the idea of eating a roasted dog on a sweltering hot Southeast Asia day with dirty hands and smelly clothes around people who have never had a bath in their life is a bit overwhelming. So what does a person do? You do what I did. You just pick up that dog, scrape off the hair, and eat it. You don't want to; you just do it. And you thank God you have food to eat and can keep it down. But you pray the whole time, "Please don't let me get sick from eating this."

The trick is in knowing when to eat it. I have some rules that I follow. Since there is no refrigeration, you want to make sure your food is fresh. If it's cold, don't eat it. (Cold is a relative term because actually nothing is cold in Southeast Asia.) If flies are on it, be careful because not only are they eating the meat, but they are also laying their eggs in it. If the food item doesn't look fresh and there are no flies on it, then by all means don't eat it. If it is too old for the flies, it is too old for you. Actually, it is probably filled with larva, and the adult flies have abandoned it so their young can feast on it.

The "Cold-Water-Showers-and-Candles" Mind-set

Some people cannot handle living on a mission field because only cold water is available, making the daily shower a memorable experience. Some cannot handle it because they have to use candles or kerosene where they live since there's no electricity. Others more commonly just cannot handle the heat or the cold. I understand these issues entirely.

As I have gotten older, I have become extremely sensitive to heat. When I prepare to go to a country, the first thing I do is research to discover what the coolest months are, and I plan my trip around those dates. When I get hot, I tend to pass out. As a diabetic, I have learned that sun and heat accelerate the burning of sugar in my blood. That's why a person can lie on the beach all day and be exhausted. Though he has done nothing, the sun has sucked the sugar right out of his bloodstream and has exhausted him. The brain feeds on blood sugar, so when a person's sugar level is dangerously low, the body begins to shut down everything unnecessary for immediate survival, including the kidneys, the liver, etc. as the brain tries to reserve all the sugar to maintain its function. Once the person passes out, if sugar is not consumed quickly, a hypoglycemic like me will go into shock, then into a coma, and then die. So I definitely understand the situation, but what I don't understand is why a missionary did not know the climate of the country before he ever raised support to go there.

I have personally known missionaries who survived deputation to arrive on the field and learn he cannot handle the heat, only to leave within two months, return home, and become a pastor. What a waste of a calling! What a waste of hundreds of thousands of missions dollars given by his supporting churches! This whole failure could have been avoided with Google and five minutes of research on that country's climate. If he had even suspected it might be too hot, why not go there to visit during the hottest month of the year to see if he can handle the climate? Of course, there is yet another solution—buy an air conditioner.

The "Armed-Guards-at-the-Grocery-Store" Mind-set

Another cultural difference that really upsets people is seeing armed guards patrolling everywhere—at the grocery store, at McDonald's, and even in their neighborhood at night. When they go to the bank, guards carry AK-47s. This show of force just scares them to death.

I have always thought that excuse to be hilarious. To me, the idea of living in a third-world country and not seeing armed guards at one of those establishments would be frightening! Having a guard means, "This is a safe place to eat." "This is a safe bank to walk into."

Not having a guard says, "You better be careful."

Well, of course, the logical thing people would then say, "Why do you want to live in a place where you have to be so concerned about your safety?"

I'm not suggesting that we do always want to live there. As a slave of the Lord Jesus Christ, I go where He tells me to go. Yes, there are times when it's dangerous, but a servant does what his Master commissions him to do. He doesn't worry about it; he just does it.

The "There's-No-Walmart" Mind-set

Some say, "Well, I just can't get what I need here." That excuse reminds me of the song, "All I want for Christmas is my two front teeth." A person can certainly live without them—although he looks much better with them!

My point is that it is absurd for a missionary to give up his service to God because the country, or his location in that country, he has chosen to live in does not have the conveniences to which he is accustomed. On most foreign fields, there are no Walmarts, no McDonald's, and no Starbucks, but there are souls there who need the Gospel. Perhaps it would be better if missionaries concentrated more on their calling and less on their convenience. Having this mind-set is not always easy, but it is always necessary. When looking back on all the struggles that missionaries have endured over the centuries, it seems silly that anyone would allow such excuses as "no Walmart" to deter them from their calling. But with some, it does.

In the first one hundred years of missionary work from England, the average lifespan of a missionary going to Africa was only six years. And the lifespan was statistically that high because one stubborn old guy refused to die and lasted 17 years! Death was such a certainty for missionaries that they began the practice of packing their clothes and belongings, not in crates—but in caskets. This was so that when the missionaries arrived in port and they were stricken with disease and death followed, the body could be buried immediately, rather than curing in the hot sun. When their churches gathered on the docks in Plymouth to say goodbye to the missionary families, they had no conceivable hope of ever seeing them again. Furlough had not yet been invented, and most would not last long enough to reach furlough anyway. In fact, many never even made it to Africa; they perished on board the ships and were buried at sea.

Whatever inconveniences a modern-day missionary must endure for the cause of Christ is nothing compared to what has already been endured by thousands who went before him. Many missionaries tend to believe they are taking up their crosses, but in reality, they have no idea what that means.

In Roman times, when the passage *"...If any man will come after me, let him...take up his cross...."* was written and the command given, the cross was never even picked up unless crucifixion was imminent. It was not carried to show a willingness to suffer; it was carried because the person was on his way to the place of execution.

A Christian today picks up his in the morning and lays it down at night, thinking he has done his Master some great service by the inconvenience of carrying it around. The prisoners in Paul's days picked up theirs and didn't lay it down until the guards standing before them had a hammer in one hand and a nail in the other.

But if life without its shopping pleasures means that much to you, then hang on. One thing I can promise you is that if you stay long enough, there will be a Starbucks, and a McDonald's, and maybe even a Walmart for you to visit one day.

❖

The "Cultural-Differences" Mind-set

As I have already stated, the mind-set that causes missionaries to quit most often is the inability to adapt to the culture. In fact, the majority of missionaries who do not return to the field after coming home for their first furlough cite cultural differences as the number-one reason for quitting. Christians need to remind themselves that there is another culture which they should be living by, and that is the culture of the Word of God—not the culture of the United States.

It doesn't matter if I cannot have turkey on Thanksgiving Day. It does not matter if I don't have a ham with those little clove spikes in it on Christmas Day. It doesn't matter if there's no Christmas tree or lights or snow or Santa Claus or anything else. Does it really matter? What does it matter if I don't get to watch the Super Bowl game? What does it matter if my neighbors look at me funny when I celebrate on the Fourth of July? It doesn't matter. All that matters is that I am where my Master told me to go—doing what my Master told me to do.

❖

The "Our-Motivation-Is-Incorrect" Mind-set

Is a missionary's intent to win the lost or to promote his own denomination, mission board, or organization? Unfortunately, I have seen times when missionaries from different boards will not even work with each other. Even though both serve with fundamental Baptist boards, they won't even fellowship together. How wrong that is! How sad! We are the body of Christ—brothers in the faith. We are to be one with each other.

Missionaries are not in the country to promote this ministry or that ministry; they are there to promote the glory of God. Missionaries should fight against any mind-set, any attitude, and any board that will prohibit or hinder them from doing that.

❖

The "Our-Calling-Is-Questioned" Mind-set

Finally, there is the nagging question that usually only comes when a missionary feels that he is a failure: "Was it God's will for me to be here or my own?" Many times people say, "I'm not sure anymore that God wanted me to come."

May I point out a thought in all tenderness? My mom told me that she always wanted to be a missionary to China—even before she was saved. My dad likewise wanted to be a missionary and turned down the opportunity because he was fearful. Before his life ended, he was traveling with me anywhere I could take him around the world and loved every minute of it.

Many people live a life of guilt because they believe they should have been a missionary and never were or they were a missionary at one time but quit. These good people beat themselves up for the rest of their lives. May I offer a suggestion? Maybe it wasn't God Who wanted you to be a missionary; maybe it was you. What do I mean?

Well, if you're like me, you grew up being encouraged to give Him your all, to do all that you can do for the Lord, and to give Him your very best. We even sang songs about giving ourselves to the cause of Christ. "Give of your best to the Master. Give of the strength of your youth..." I am convinced that many who really wanted to serve the Lord, but maybe had not truly received a calling from God, volunteered for missionary work and then confused that willingness to serve and please Him as being a calling.

In other words, because some Christians wanted to serve God and give Him their very best and since they had been brought up to believe that being a missionary was the zenith of giving their best to God, that nothing could be a greater calling than that, they therefore decided to be a missionary. They didn't hear any sirens going off or see any warning lights flashing, so they thought God must be okay with their decision. After all, they saw a video and now have a burden for those people. So these good Christians became missionaries. But after getting to the country and enduring all the things that they have experienced and not achieving the total salvation of the country, they grow depressed and question whether or not they were really called by God.

I want to encourage missionaries who find themselves in these circumstances. I don't want them to beat themselves up or to beat up anybody else for that matter. At least they went or were willing to go. At least they gave missions a try, and in doing so, they came to the conclusion that it was not what God had for them.

May I affirm that you are not a bad or disobedient Christian? You should be honored for what you did while the rest of us stayed at home and built bigger barns. At least you gave it a shot. My hat's off to each and every one of you. I know this about you: you will, in a dedicated manner, support missions and missionaries for the rest of your life. I say God bless you.

❖

The "Our-Fields-Are-Closed" Mind-set

Much is made about the exclusion of sending or providing a witness in lands that are closed to the Gospel, and rightfully so. However, another speed bump in world evangelism is the ever-growing list of nations that are considered to be "open" but "restricted." By that I do not mean lands where entering covertly or as a businessman or English teacher is required. I am referring to lands that are open to missionaries but restrict their work due to legal reasons. There are many missionaries in Brazil for example, but they are barred legally from working among the tribal groups. In fact, even Brazilian preachers are not legally allowed to approach them. The influence of anthropologists in the United Nations has convinced the "modern" world that a disservice is done by making contact with the primitive tribes because in doing so, their clothing, their hygiene, their living methods, etc. are changed, and eventually they lose their language, their culture, and their traditions. This argument presents a valid point.

When Missionary John Paton first went to the New Hebrides Islands in the South Pacific, he feared that he would follow the fate of the missionaries who preceded him in that region and be forced to give his life for the Gospel. When he buried his wife and newborn child, he had to literally sleep on their graves to keep the natives from digging up their bodies and eating them. Of his 35 years there, he later testified that he did not know of a single native that had not made a profession of faith in Jesus Christ. Many years passed with threats and difficulties, but when he finally passed away, the natives placed an inscribed altar to remember his work among them. It read simply, "When John Paton arrived, there were no Christians; when he died, there were no cannibals." Some things in primitive cultures need to be changed.

As a student of history and anthropology, I have a tendency to agree with the experts, but my humanity, shaped by my faith, overcomes the nostalgia of preserving primitive cultures. After all, who are we to deny progress, medical care, science and education, not to mention the Word of God to an entire ethnic group—whether it be the last surviving member of a tribe or just one of thousands who live in deep jungles, forgotten by man and unexposed to civilization. How would we feel if the sandal was on the other foot?

However, what I am speaking of is a totally different matter. I am referring to nations that are open and friendly to the missionary and eager for the good that always follows the Gospel. There is a new wind blowing around the world that is spreading a fire that no one seems able to extinguish. The country of Panama is an example of that change which is just beginning to be noticed by the sending churches but is already affecting the lives of missionaries. What is it? Many nations are now changing their laws requiring how often and where a missionary (or any tourist) can stay in their land and how they have to arrange departure if they are to be allowed to reenter.

In the past, a missionary family merely had to leave the country, usually every three months. For families like mine when we lived in Honduras, that meant that every three months we had to drive across the border into either Guatemala, El Salvador, or Nicaragua, and have our passports stamped that we left Honduras and entered another country. After driving across the border, we could make a U-turn, have that country stamp our passports again as we were leaving, then drive through "immigration" on the Honduran side of the border and have our passports stamped for "reentry" for another three months.

This trek took a day out of our schedules. Of course, to be honest, because I was a legal resident, I didn't have to do this, and because of my "contacts" in the government, neither did my family. But generally, missionaries don't have such contacts because they are taught to only reach and meet the poor, either by instruction or by example. To our disadvantage, we tend to avoid the wealthy or militarily connected as if they had the plague.

Panama used to be the same way, but now, like Honduras and many other countries, they require the missionary to stay out of their country from three days to two weeks before returning. That now means that the missionary has to leave his work for an extended period every 90 days. He must also endure the added financial burden of many nights in a motel and eating at restaurants. Some see this as a "mini-vacation" every three months. Others see it as an interruption to their ministry and work. Another glitch is that the government of Panama (like many other countries) now requires the missionary not only to leave the country, but he must return to his own sending country before being allowed to return again to Panama. Thus every three months, the missionary must purchase round-trip airline tickets for each member of his family, plus pay for the added expenses of hotel, food, and car rental. Most cannot bear this added financial burden, and their supporting churches see this as the final straw as far as funding goes, since it will add (for a missionary couple with two children) an added budget need of $3,000 to $4,000 every three months. (And let's be realistic about the numbers. When was the last time you met a missionary who had only two children?) The end result is that the missionary quits his field and comes home—usually for good.

Photo: Our team of Indians and Americans went to this village to expose them to the knowledge of God. Many were converted that day, and eventually a church was planted among this tribal group.
[Photo taken January 2008]

Fixing
the
Problem

Global Harvest

If the ratio of Christian workers to total population that exists in North Africa were applied to the United States and Canada, these two countries would only have about 120 full-time Christian workers living in them. Also, there would be only 7 small churches in both the United States and Canada combined.

Statistical Data
on Unreached People Groups

- 865 million unreached Muslims or Islamic followers in 3,330 cultural sub-groupings
- 550 million unreached Hindus in 1,660 cultural sub-groups
- 150 million unreached Chinese in 830 groups
- 275 million unreached Buddhists in 900 groups
- 2,550 unreached tribal groups (which are mainly animistic) with a total population of 140 million
- Forming a smaller, though important, unreached group are the 17 million Jews scattered across 134 countries

Introduction

Did you know that one out of ten people on the earth is an illiterate Indian?

U p to this point, I have mainly addressed the problems missionaries face and why they face them. From this point on, I would like to concentrate more on the solutions. There will always be problems, but solutions cannot be far behind if there is to be success.

In Bible college I did not learn much, but what I did learn has stayed with me. I remember Dr. Wendell Evans once teaching about counseling and suggesting a method to help get to the bottom of any situation. It went something like this:

- What is the problem?
- What is the cause?
- What are the root causes?
- What are the solutions?
- What is the best solution?
- What steps need to be taken to accomplish the solution?

So please allow me to use this method and logic to address the problem in missions.

Question

What is the problem?

Answer

We are falling behind in evangelizing the world.

Question

What is the cause?

Answer

Not enough missionaries are going out to reach the entire world.

Question

What are the root causes?

Answer

- We have had a prejudice against supporting the national preachers.
- The next generation of missionaries is not being properly trained on Biblical principles and practices in missions.
- The youth are not being recruited to replace the elderly, dying, and retiring missionaries to even keep up with the numbers, much less shrink them.

Question

What are the solutions and/or the best solutions? I believe there are two joint solutions.

Answer

- Encourage believers and churches to support more national preachers.
- Train our next generation with Biblical principles and cultural methods to reach their targeted ethnic groups.
- Encourage our youth to "get their feet wet" with missions through short-term trips to open their eyes to the adventure and the supremacy of missions as a service to God.

Question

What steps should be taken to accomplish the solutions?

Answer

- In regard to the nationals, provide believers and churches with the opportunity to personally support a national church planter based on his lifestyle, ministry experience, doctrine, integrity, and accountability. That goal has been accomplished with Final Frontiers and a half-dozen other similar ministries which Final Frontiers has helped to launch.
- In regard to the next generation of missionaries, train

them, train them, and train them. The days of a missionary's being a man who couldn't make it as a pastor is over. Missionary specialists, like the Navy SEALS, need to be developed to once again make missions a coveted ministry that is reserved for the elite of God's servants— not the incompetent. Final Frontiers is doing just that with our School of Missions and our Missionary Training Programs that are designed to offer a master's level, two-year course that takes place on a minimum of three continents.

- In regard to involving the American youth, develop a ministry that will expose them to the mission field for a week or two, at the very least. This mission trip is designed to wake them up to the need of the world and to their ability to personally satisfy that need, to recruit serious youth to become missionaries, and to provide in-depth, hands-on mentoring in missions. Final Frontiers has done this with our High Calling Adventure Trips.

Today's young people get upset because they break a fingernail or didn't get the right designer clothes for Christmas or don't have enough minutes on their cell phone to send the required number of daily texts. Let them spend a week on the field, and they won't even miss the phone. A "text" will cease to be a synonym of "chat" and will once again mean "a portion of a book." Their designer clothes will be ripped and muddy, and the very thought of the money they wasted on them will cause them to be ashamed of their former "lust of the eyes and pride of life," and those clothes will probably be given away to another national teen before they leave the country. When they get home, they will probably still look like the kids you sent, but they won't talk like they used to talk anymore. They won't act like they used to act anymore. Young people who go on a mission trip generally become a new creation.

Did you know that 818 unevangelized ethno linguistic peoples have never been targeted by any Christian agencies?

Did you know that organized Christianity has total contact with 3,590 religions but no contact at all with 353 other religions and their over 500 million adherents?

CHAPTER 1

Fixing Problem One: Support National Church Planters

Did you know that each day an average of 50,000 people in China die, and in India another 40,000 perish? Most of these do so without having heard the Gospel even once.

B y now, I think if you are still with me, you know that Final Frontiers exists to support national church planters in third-world countries.

With all the missionaries eager to serve, one might wonder why Final Frontiers specializes in supporting national church planters rather than in sending American church planters (missionaries).

In fact, Final Frontiers does send some, and as time marches on, their numbers will increase. However, Final Frontiers has a standard for missionaries that goes far beyond a simple pastoral recommendation and a pedigree from an approved Bible college.

And though I will touch on that toward the end of my writing, let me begin now with a brief explanation of why Final Frontiers supports national preachers.

The Obvious Benefits of Supporting
a National Church Planter

Citizenship

Over 40 percent of all nations are currently closed to the traditional foreign missionary, and that number is expected to continue to increase. Yet in reality, these nations are never closed to the national preacher. He has citizenship! When a country "closes its doors" to the missionary, the national preacher has merely been "locked in," providing him with a "captive audience."

Language

For the national preacher, there is no "down time" spent in learning a new language, whereas language training comprises a large portion of the foreign missionary's first term. Most national preachers are bilingual or multilingual. Many will speak five, ten, or even more languages of the tribal peoples within their regions, whereas the foreign missionary is usually taught to learn only the "official" language. The detriment of this language deficit is seen clearly in nations such as India, where there are more than 1,600 different languages and dialects used, in addition to the "official" language.

Culture

The national preacher is "at home" in his nation and experiences no cultural strain. It has been estimated that over 50 percent of all missionaries do not return for a second term of duty. The primary reason given for this is "the inability to adapt to the culture."

Furlough

Furlough is not necessary in order for the national preacher to maintain an accountability with his sponsors. In fact, the funds that would be used to bring him to America for furlough could instead be used to build a church building or even to support his family and ministry for two to five years or longer. Because of this benefit, he does not suffer the 20 percent down time experienced by foreign missionaries who are required to spend one year out of every five on furlough.

Retirement

Retirement is not an option for the national preacher. Currently, over 50 percent of all American missionaries are at least 55 years old. Many of these servants of God will face mandatory retirement within the next ten years. Unfortunately, not enough young missionaries are stepping forward to replace this retiring army of experienced servants. The reality of mandatory retirement based upon age is an American cultural concept, little known and less understood by national preachers in other lands who view their calling as one of lifetime ministry.

Time

While many missionaries are paid a salary by their board or denomination, the average missionary who is involved with a "faith mission," spends 2.5 years or more raising their financial support. Every national preacher supported by Final Frontiers is already "on the field" and actively involved in church planting, with or without regular monthly support. With the help of a sponsor, they can dramatically accelerate their efforts.

Economics

The average personal and work-related support needed for a foreign missionary is $5,000 to $9,000 per month, depending on his field of service. This level of support is required because foreigners typically live at a higher standard than do the nationals, and they must have funding for "necessary" items that the national would never dream of owning. Worldwide, the average support needed for the national preacher is only about

$100 monthly. When inflation rises, his standard of living remains equal to those among whom he ministers. In short, for what it takes to support the typical foreign missionary for one month, the typical national preacher can be supported for more than five years!

How National Preachers Are Approved for Support

The approval process for a preacher is a lengthy one. Let me explain the process.

Final Frontiers' method of discovery is to work through an established organizational structure in foreign countries that already has an accountability system in place. Final Frontiers desires to support men who are held highly accountable for their doctrine, lifestyle, ministry, and family life. We never consider a "lone ranger" for support.

The final approval for support is based upon several factors, including:

- Introduction
- Doctrine
- Morality
- Family life
- Ministry experience

Introduction

The preacher being considered for support must be recommended to Final Frontiers by either a Western missionary from an established, fundamental board, or by a national pastor in whom confidence has been placed due to his doctrinal stand, etc. The recommendation must be based upon a long-term, personal knowledge of that preacher and his ministry. It is not enough to "know of" the man; the one recommending him must have known him directly, and for some time, to be able to vouch for his qualification. Any applications coming to the Final Frontiers home office must be approved by the national director. Otherwise, these applications will be returned to the country of origin so that the national director can get to know the preacher and consider him for support at some time in the future. This process is also aided by regional directors and tribal directors, who would be in a position to know men that the national director may not know. Nevertheless, the same criteria for approval applies. Before the national director sends an application to Final Frontiers, he first examines the applicant according to the above-listed categories that are detailed as follows.

If at any time a director forwards an application that is not qualified, he forfeits his right to recommend any others in the future, regardless of how long he has worked with Final Frontiers or how many qualified and outstanding preachers he has recommended in the past. This is what we at Final Frontiers call our "one-strike-and-you're-out" policy.

Doctrine

Before the applicant receives Final Frontiers' doctrinal statement, he must first submit his own. Sometimes these are lengthy and detailed; other times they are very simple and general. This composition is usually due to a lack of formal education, but by no means implies a lack of zeal, knowledge, or devotion to doctrinal purity. Our basic intention is to learn if the preacher is fundamental in his doctrine. We make no attempt to require the preacher to use a particular denominational title, but his doctrine must be in accord with sound fundamental Biblical teaching. It should be noted that denominational names carry much more weight in the American culture than in other cultures around the world.

In tribal groups particularly, while these Christians may possess the same doctrine, they may have never heard of such designations as Baptist, Methodists, etc. Oftentimes they just refer to themselves as "Christians," taking the example from the book of Acts. This choice of names is done innocently, without the awareness that the term "Christian" is used as a denominational name in the United States. In other cases, denominational teachings may vary from one country to another. For instance Baptists in the United States firmly believe in the doctrine of "eternal security"; however, Baptists in Eastern Europe typically do not. Therefore, the applicant's beliefs are determined by his doctrinal position and preaching, rather than by his ministry's name. It should also be noted that Final Frontiers does not support men who are hired as denominational staff. While such men may be needy, they should request help from their employers. Final Frontiers supports only men who, though plugged in to a local accountability structure, are independent ministers and not controlled by a denomination.

Morality

The New Testament books of Timothy and Titus provide God's qualifications for a man in the ministry. Final Frontiers seeks to affirm that the applicant meets these same qualifications. A careful study of these books provide a greater clarity of the character and quality of the men being supported.

One such important characteristic is the preacher's testimony with those both in and out of the church. Therefore, it is important not only for the preacher to be morally pure, but to be known as a morally pure man, both by believers and nonbelievers alike.

Family Life

Because the one recommending the preacher has a long-term, personal knowledge of the applicant, he also has an equally good knowledge of the preacher's family. Thus, a determination is drawn that the applicant's wife is a faithful and good example to the women in her community. The children are also required to follow in the faith of their father. It is further determined whether or not he is the husband of one wife, as polygamy is a common practice throughout the world. In some cultures, polygamy is not only legal but encouraged.

Ministry Experience

Final Frontiers never supports a man who "intends" to do something once he receives funds. Support is only given to those who, by faith and at a personal sacrifice, are already "doing it." Additionally, Final Frontiers does not support full-time students who have not had an opportunity to prove themselves and are therefore still novices. While it is the hope and aim of Final Frontiers to assist the preacher in continuing education, he must be a preacher first and a student second. After receiving a diploma, many theological students in third-world nations decide to go into business rather than the ministry. Our policy guarantees that no money will be "wasted" in this way. A student may be sponsored only if he is actively and personally involved in church planting. This man then is not considered a truly "full-time" student by our standards, as are many seminary students in America who do no ministry until after graduation.

In short, Final Frontiers requires that the men who receive support be veteran ministers who are involved in church planting and discipleship. Often their applications imply they have not started a church or discipled another preacher, but it is because of cultural misunderstandings between the languages. You see, in most cases, a man will work with a team of others in church planting and discipleship. This team is always led by a more experienced pastor who, in their eyes, "gets the credit." Thus, while their application may state they have not started a church, it has been determined through personal interviews by the tribal, regional, and national directors that they have indeed been involved with a team of men doing so and therefore do have experience.

Final Words of Explanation

A dossier is gathered on each man who is recommended to Final Frontiers for support. The sponsor should be aware that the existence of this man's dossier certifies he has survived years of scrutiny and examination of his life, morals, doctrine, and ministry; and he has passed with high marks. It has also been determined that he is in need of financial assistance because of the ever-expanding scope of his ministry, the economic situation of his nation, and the poverty of the national churches in general.

While the men who are supported may be pastors, they are in reality church planters, and as such, forego financial stability. Let me explain. After a church is planted and able to support a pastor, rather than remaining in that established work, he moves on to begin another work. Because of this objective, he will most likely always be in need of support, unless his status changes to that of a sedentary pastor. Some of the men who receive support pastor a single church, but they are also involved in reaching out to other villages with the Gospel. Thus, while some funds will be used for food and clothing, a great portion of the funds will be used for transportation and tools for preaching the Gospel.

Most preachers require only one or two sponsors to subsidize their ministry, but some, because of their nation's economy or ministry travels, require three or four. To obtain information about a certain pastor's support status, call the Final Frontiers ministry office before sending a larger check than originally agreed upon. It may be that this pastor already has an additional sponsor. If you have any questions, please feel free to inquire.

❖

The Application Process

The preachers supported by Final Frontiers are sometimes recommended by missionaries or by pastors in the United States who have personal knowledge of them. But more often than not, they are recommended by others who currently receive sponsorship monies. The recommendation must be based upon "a long-term personal knowledge" of the recommended preacher and his ministry. Regardless of the initial contact, each man must be approved before the work on his sponsorship can begin.

The process begins by the individual's completing an application which asks general questions regarding his family life and background. I have listed sample questions which will help Final Frontiers get to know the man personally and to assist in the compilation of a short biography on him and his family. All of this gleaned information helps develop a portfolio to be used in raising sponsorship for him.

- What is your given name and by what name are you called?
- How long have you been married?
- Are all your children followers of Christ?
- What is your home built of?
- Is it consistent with others in your community?
- Are you a member of a tribal group? If so, which one?
- How many languages do you speak? What are they?
- What is your income and who provides it?

From these kinds of questions, the questionnaire focuses on more specific ministry questions such as:

- How many churches have you personally started?
- What percentage of your converts receive baptism?
- How many men have you trained for the ministry?
- What are the names of those men currently being trained?
- In what other types of ministry are you involved?
- Who trained you for the ministry?

Doctrinal statements are exchanged, and the national pastor confirms that he is in agreement with it on all points. Finally, Final Frontiers asks for a complete written testimony of his life and ministry. This information, along with a letter of recommendation is forwarded to the national preacher in charge of gathering data (referred to as the national director). He collects this information as well as all future quarterly reports if the national pastor is approved for support. When the file on a potential candidate for sponsorship is complete and he has been thoroughly examined, that file is sent to the international office for publishing and consideration by potential sponsors.

It is Final Frontiers' stated policy not to support men who are employed by a denomination, as their support comes from such. Rather, Final Frontiers seeks to assist independent preachers, accountable to a local church, fellowship, and/or association who believe as we do and have no one but God to turn to for assistance. As He directs us to them, we find ourselves in a position to be the answer to their prayers.

It is also the policy of Final Frontiers to support only veteran preachers who are currently serving and perpetually involved in church planting and discipleship, not full-time students or those waiting for payment in order to serve. These men must live a Biblically separated lifestyle, have full submission to the Word of God as their sole and final authority, and conform to the requirements given in the New Testament to qualify for ministry.

❖

The Interview Process

Once the initial application has been approved for further consideration, the preacher will then undergo a series of interviews.

First, he meets with the preacher responsible for oversight in his particular geographic area or ministry type. For lack of a specific term, hereafter this man will be referred to as an "overseer." This is not a supervisory position, but rather an accountability function. Such men are usually the recognized leaders of a group of preachers. (Ministry type refers to various ministries such as tribal, radio, leper, Bible translation, etc.) If the overseer made the recommendation for support, then his letter of recommendation is equivalent to an interview in that such a recommendation is not made without a long-term, personal knowledge of the man and his ministry.

Upon a successful interview with the overseer, the national

pastor's application and interview records are forwarded to the national director. Such men are usually free to travel throughout their areas at least once each quarter. At that time, the national director meets with the preacher and his family to examine their lifestyle, ministry, and personal life.

At any point in the interview process, a preacher's application can be rejected due to any flaw which may be discovered in his doctrine, personality, lifestyle, or ministry experience, past or present. If, however, he passes both interviews successfully, his application and all pertinent data are held at the national director's office (church) until such time as the director presents the application and photographs with his approval to the home office. This man's story is published in the form of a portfolio, and a sponsor (or sponsors) is sought for him.

❖

The Preacher's Accountability

In order for each preacher to maintain a level of accountability, Final Frontiers requires a report to be completed every trimester. Guidelines are given to the preacher on the type of information that he needs to gather. Such reports are sent to the overseer or to the national director for translation into English. Then they are mailed to the international office in America. After the report is copied, the original is sent to the preacher's sponsor. If the preacher does not have a specific sponsor, his reports are placed in his file, which further expands his portfolio. These files are maintained for the future sponsor.

Generally, if the preacher fails to send a quarterly report, his support is withheld until the report is received. Some exceptions can be made due to geographic or political barriers which can cause unexpected interference. In such cases, reports are expected to be forwarded at the time of the receipt of funds. If a pattern persists in a preacher's failing to report on time, a decision will be made after investigation by the regional director and national director, as to whether or not the preacher's support should be suspended permanently.

Some men, in countries such as China or Tibet or in remote jungle areas, are cut off from contact for three months to a year at a time. In such cases, it is obvious that trimester contact is impossible. Thus, exceptions can be made with the sponsor's consent.

Frequent trips are made to the countries where support is offered. This enables Final Frontiers to remain current with the preachers in an intimate way and serves to inform us in regard to the needs they have, which their culture may not permit them to share. This contact further serves as an opportunity for them to counsel with us in regard to needed changes in policy. Furthermore, it provides time to gather data and interview prospective applicants.

Such trips also serve as opportunities for preachers and laymen whose churches support this ministry to visit the field and to examine for themselves the quality and character of the men for whom sponsorships are raised.

Accountability is a two-lane street: the national preachers to Final Frontiers and Final Frontiers to the sponsor. Furthermore, that accountability involves more than just finances alone. It includes areas such as character, lifestyle, doctrine, work ethics, and family life. In short, they must be faithful to the Lord in their ministries and faithful in turning in their reports. Final Frontiers must, in turn, be faithful to the sponsor in our solicitation of funds and dissemination of information. Finally, Final Frontiers must be faithful to the preacher, dispersing his funds in full and on time.

How Accountability Is Maintained for the Sponsor

"Accountability is everything" is one of the precepts by which Final Frontiers lives. If a person cannot provide an acceptable level of accountability, he should not receive support. A person's stewardship does not end when a check is dropped in the offering plate; to the contrary, that is where it begins. The following outlines Final Frontiers' simple, but effective, steps of accountability, which I have been told are unmatched by any mission board.

Approval of the National Board

In each nation, an advisory and accountability board, consisting of the spiritual leaders and peers of the national preachers and chosen from among the preachers themselves, is appointed to determine, recommend, oversee and maintain an accountability between the preacher, the international office, and their sponsors. Their recommendations of approval and, if necessary, dismissal are absolute.

Continuing Accountability

National and regional directors are appointed from among the members of the advisory and accountability boards of each nation. Such directors maintain a local accountability in the areas of doctrine, morals, and ministry. They also verify all (required) trimester reports for accuracy before they are translated and sent to their respective sponsors. These reports are required for continued support, unless hindered by geographic or political reasons. In addition, the directors oversee the distribution of cameras which are available to all sponsored preachers for use in documenting their ministries.

Visionary Trips

Pastors and sponsors are encouraged to accompany Final Frontier staff members on frequent announced (and unannounced) trips in order to insure accountability. This ministry believes that accountability is the key to any successful ministry, but having the missionary in a church once every five years to speak for thirty minutes is not accountability. Accountability would be better accomplished by churches sending a representative to the field to see for himself the work of the missionary being supported—whether that ministry be the work of a national preacher or a foreign missionary.

Did you know that 124 million new souls begin life on Earth each year, but Christianity's 4,000 foreign mission agencies baptize only 4 million new person a year?

CHAPTER 2

Fixing Problem Two: Biblically Training American Missionaries

Did you know that in Islamic North Africa, there is only one Christian pastor or missionary for every two million people?

In ancient days, the student did not choose where he would study; rather, the instructor chose the student. Paul was tutored by Gamaliel; Aristotle tutored Alexander the Great, and so forth. My goal is to mentor, to train, and to evaluate the missionary candidate in order to determine those who could be invited to join the Final Frontiers ministry. This tutoring would be conducted not only by me, but also by the Final Frontiers staff in the United States and abroad and by various proven, effective missionaries as well as a host of national preachers.

During the training, the men would be learning the methods used by Final Frontiers; proprietary software; how to plant churches in rural, urban, and tribal settings; how to establish and operate feeding centers; and how to start church-based Bible institutes, etc. Additionally, if these men are accepted as a Final Frontiers missionary associate, they would also be raising support for national preachers and children, for Bible smuggling, for camels used in transportation, etc. while they are on deputation or furlough.

In reality, Final Frontiers does not want a "board" per se. What I have designed is an "Association of Foreign Missionaries" who agree with the Final Frontiers philosophy and wish to work hand in hand with us. They would be independent, but Final Frontiers would handle their funds and act as their board, while exercising no control over them. They would be referred to as "associate missionaries," and we already have a few. They would go out under our banner, using our name and promoting our ministry. We, in turn, promote them, help finance their work, process their funds and reports, and guarantee rescue operations for them and their family, if necessary. These missionaries would not be left alone on the field. Many boards do not do this, but they should. We will and do negotiate, using the means at our disposal, and because of our accumulated histories and contacts, those methods are legion (and confidential).

❖

Affiliate Missionaries

Final Frontiers also has what are called "affiliate missionaries." These men serve under a different fundamental board, but they serve as regional directors for Final Frontiers by distributing funds and reports, returning reports to the office, and qualifying new men for support. Final Frontiers works with many of these regional directors, but sometimes their boards may not prefer it. Generally, we are building their ministries by supporting their preachers so they don't have to.

Years ago we began working with missionary Randall Stirewalt of the Baptist Bible Fellowship in Eldoret, Kenya. At that time Randall had been serving for some 20 years and had become discouraged because he had ONLY started 12 churches. Amazing humility! He was actually at the point of quitting over what he wrongly perceived as failure. Final Frontiers began supporting his trained, experienced preachers, and over the years their numbers have grown. Now some 18 years later, the number of churches Randall has been able to lead his Kenyan church planters to start has swollen from 12 to more than several hundred—all because his men were subsidized! Those sponsorships allowed the national pastors to become full-time in church planting ministries.

Final Frontiers begins by trying to build in the missionary's heart the reality of the calling God has given him. Missionaries should not be failed pastors or novice youth. Age does not make a missionary an expert, nor does his board. A missionary should be a Spartan in spiritual warfare, a Barnabas in his care for the body, a Daniel in his wisdom, a Joseph in his administrative capabilities, a Paul in his zeal, and a "mighty man" in his exploits for God. He should be both a student and a scholar; and he should possess superior knowledge in culture, history, politics, and geography in his given land, surpassing that of the educated national citizen. He should be the epitome of "becoming all things to all men." Missionaries are not born; they are trained and evolve from a combination of desire, failures, suffering, tragedies, heartbreak, humility, and experience.

To assist in developing such men, who like their predecessors are capable of "turning the world upside down," Final Frontiers has begun to develop a program that will equate to a master's degree in Missiology. This master's is primarily based not on academics, but on experience, exposure to other cultures, and mentoring by experienced, successful missionaries and national church leaders.

This program would be a two-year course that takes place in the United States (only slightly) and in at least three other continents, providing exposure to various countries on each continent. For example:

- Asia—Thailand, Cambodia and/or Myanmar
- Africa—Ghana, Kenya and/or Ivory Coast
- Latin America—Honduras, Guatemala and/or Peru
- Middle East—confidential
- Europe—Romania, Ukraine and/or Lithuania

In each country or continent, the master's students would serve

232 The Great Omission

and be mentored by tribal, national, rural, and urban pastors as well as by experienced and successful foreign missionaries. The students would be exposed to ministry philosophies, local food, weather, traditions, and root cultures of each region and tribe. They would serve for at least one month in each location.

❖

Other Courses of Basic Study

- **Ethnography**—the study of cultures

This class will equip the missionary in getting to know the cultures with which he will come in contact. Gaining an understanding to their culture builds immediate respect and acceptance into the hearts of the citizens, as the missionary will likely know more about them than they know about themselves. The class will also give the student the key to unlock the Gospel in their culture, as every culture has glimpses of the Truth contained in their language or history.

- **Anthropology**—the study of human (tribal) origin, behavior, culture, and interaction with other people groups

In this class the missionary will determine why a society acts as it does toward each other and toward outsiders. Studying anthropology will enable the student to know how to best communicate the Gospel and how to point out the strengths and weaknesses of engrained culture to the new believers and church leaders. For example, Asian cultures have a deep respect—even to the point of worship—of their elderly. Their knowing that this respect is a parallel Biblical doctrine opens the door to more exposure to the Word of God.

- **Cartography**—the science of mapping specializing in the use of demographics and geographic analysis

The missionary will be taught to map neighborhoods and regions based on the local demographics and identify who lives there—the tribes, the cultures, the languages, the available places, and the population by age groups, gender, income, etc. The data can, in many cases, be uploaded to

Google Earth, allowing on-campus, undergraduate students to view and analyze the information as well and to assist the missionary with his work.

• **Practical Immersion**—how to adapt to cultures in order to blend in and become one with them (e.g., becoming a "national")

• **Biblical Contextualization**—how to apply God's Word and Truth to the culture being dealt with (e.g., explaining the Biblical phrase "whiter than snow" to those living along the equator who have never seen snow)

• **Counter Surveillance**—teaches the missionary how to be observant to the potential of kidnapping, hostage taking, and assassination

• **Protective Intelligence**—steps to take to prevent a kidnapping

• **Espionage**—methods of covert operations applied to evangelizing, rescuing, gathering information, encryption, etc.

• **Basic Medicine**

• **Language Adaptation and Learning**

• **Basic Construction**—learning how to build from naturally available resources such as mud, straw, dung, sticks, rocks; how to construct an adobe stove, dig a well, etc.

• **Survival Techniques**—learning how to survive in all areas—jungle, desert, mountain, rural, and urban

• **Deputation and Accountability**—how to raise funds and how to properly report to supporters with an aim of increasing their burden, not just imparting information

• **Video and Publishing**—Using the tools to enhance ministry presentation and reporting

In addition to all of these prescribed courses of study, there will be numerous reading assignments that correlate with the subject, as well as missionary biographies and cultural histories.

Finally, each missionary will be taught the basics of several occupations so that, if necessary, he has something to fall back on in a crisis or to use as a cover. These trades could include carpentry, barbering, computer repair, or whatever the student finds interesting. This practice was customary among the Jews and was practiced by the Apostle Paul when needed while he was serving as a missionary. Mentors in the United States or abroad will be located to accomplish this purpose.

CHAPTER 3

Fixing Problem Three: Preparing for the Future

Did you know that 95 percent of the people living in the 10/40 Window are unevangelized? Many have never heard the Gospel message even once.

Preparing for the future is time sensitive; if you wait too long, the future is already past. You are then left with regrets rather than rewards.

The future is our youth. Many parents' idea of preparing their youth for a lifetime of service is to send them to summer camp and have a weekly or monthly activity for them to enjoy. And of course, activity means fun—not ministry.

When I was a teenager, my youth pastor was John Reynolds, the lifelong right arm of Curtis Hutson. John never told us what to do; rather, he instilled in us the desire to do something—anything—then he stood back and watched us get it done. If needed, he would step in with advice, but usually only when he was asked. He had a way of giving us advice and making us think the idea was ours. He was and still is a genius who looks for someone to build while most look for others who can help them build.

In looking back on those days, John really didn't care how

long the guys wore their hair, to what kind of music we listened, if we went to a movie, or if we even went mixed swimming. At least if he did, he never displayed that to me. What he cared about was that we read the Bible, loved the Lord and each other, and sought to glorify Christ. Strangely, all the other things just fell into place. His influence was so great that many of us would, after being up late on dates the night before, meet at the church at 7:00 a.m. to pray for an hour for our pastor and the services of the day.

Most of the young men with whom I grew up are in the ministry today; most of the girls are married to a preacher or missionary. Those who are not, to my knowledge, are faithful Christians serving in their home churches. What an influence John Reynolds had!

I may make some readers uncomfortable with what I am about to say (what a shocker!), but I hope you will discern my intentions as you read. In decades past, sometimes in their zeal to train up their children in the way they should go, parents confused the point. If a father trains his son to be a swimmer and that boy falls in love with the sport, his father will not need to tell him to cut his hair. His son will do so voluntarily in order to increase the speed of his laps in the pool. In fact, he may even shave his legs and arms.

Parents sometimes taught their children by example that changing the outside is what makes a man a dedicated Christian. As they grew older and decided they wanted to look a little different than how they were reared, these young adults automatically thought they were in sin. They grew to failure—not because their hearts were not right but because their hearts had been infected with too much concern for the outward appearance and not enough for the inner man.

I find it interesting that every major problem our Lord had during His ministry emanated from the Pharisees—not the Sadducees. This should not have been the case since He openly referred to His coming resurrection, and the Sadducees did not believe in such. The Pharisees, a much smaller religious group than the Sadducees, were His constant "thorn in the flesh," picking at everything He said and did, accusing Him of heresy, blasphemy, and contempt for the Judaistic faith. These Pharisees literally stood out in the crowd because of their appearance—not because of their faith. And by the way, though all the sects were religious, only one of them felt they were better, more knowledgeable, and more holy than the rest—the Pharisees. Of course the word Pharisee is not an English word. The name of their sect came from a verb in their own language. The word or name *Pharisee* literally means—are you ready for this?—are you sure?—"separated."

I hope you realize that I am not attacking standards. What I am concerned with is the emphasis put on the outside rather than the inside. This is the same message our Lord taught, and some believers have ignored it in our day—just as the "separated" did in His day. What a shame! His way is always better, always prosperous, and always successful. Our ways have emptied our pews. His ways, back when they were being followed, made ours the largest and fastest growing churches in all 50 states.

One of the most dedicated youth groups on the planet is the Mormons. Their young men spend two years of their lives as missionaries. Of course, they do have an ulterior motive; they want to become a god with their own universe. But we Christians have a stronger motive; we want to serve our God and expand His Kingdom.

The Mormon youth return home with an understanding of the world and its people. They have a zeal for missions that we don't understand. Did you know that they don't have to raise support to go? If you are a Mormon and have a house, you are expected to provide lodging for them. Their family and friends and their home "church" are required to provide for their expenses. Amazing!

Why don't we Christians who have the right message do

that? Why don't we encourage our youth when they graduate from high school to spend two years, one year, six months, or even two weeks on a mission field somewhere? Any missionary would be delighted to provide food and lodging in exchange for work. National families and preachers would be delighted to host them, as long as they could pay for their own food. They too would learn about the world and its people. They would have a burden to reach the world. Those who enter business would immediately be consumed with expanding to the country where they developed lifelong friends and have dozens of contacts. This would provide jobs for national believers who can tithe and support their own pastors.

It's logical, but it's not done. Instead, we teach our kids that the summer before college is their last opportunity to "have fun" and spend time with their friends. We don't instill eternity in their hearts; thus, they don't think about it, nor do they support it by supporting missions. They consume their income on themselves until they have their own family, and then they consume it on their family. God gets the leftovers—if there are any. To nip this problem in the bud, Final Frontiers has developed two youth-oriented trips that are geared to capture the hearts of young people for missions.

High Calling Adventure Trips

The High Calling Adventure Trips are designed to take youth on a rugged, camping/evangelistic trip for a week. The young people learn how to contend with nature, cook their own food, and hike to villages that have no roads leading to them. They live without electricity, wash their clothes in a river or stream, and have the time of their lives.

Visionary Trips

The Visionary Trips are really for all ages. It is an opportunity not so much to do, but to see the world and gain a burden for it. Over half of those who travel with us each summer are coming back for their second, third or fourth trip. We must be doing something right!

These trips are provided to open the eyes of the youth to the possibility of missionary service and, if nothing else, to burden them for the world so that as tithing church members and leaders of the future, they will understand the need and know the solution.

Missionaries in Training

Both the High Calling Adventure Trips and the Visionary Trips provides Final Frontiers with the opportunity to examine those who attend, to determine their potential as a missionary, and then to invite them to participate in our School of Missions and Missionary-in-Training program. After spending two years in this program; living and serving in urban, rural, and tribal settings on three continents; and having planted churches in at least three countries and discipled other young men to serve as they do, they are then certified as a missionary, and they are turned loose to return home and start deputation. Yes, you read it right—to start deputation! I know that most missionaries are taught that deputation comes first, but if you have never done anything, why should a church support you to do something you have never done?

Imagine when one of our approved missionaries visits a church asking for support. He has already served on three continents, learned to speak several languages, started two or more churches, and has men serving in the ministry whom he won to Christ and discipled. With him is a portfolio of photos of his work, report forms, and letters from dozens of national pastors asking churches to support him so he can return and continue his help among them. The pastor can then compare that portfolio to all the other missionary candidates who taught a junior boys' Sunday school class for a year and drove a bus. Which one would you choose to support?

Did you know that it costs Christians 700 times more money to baptize converts in rich World C countries (like Switzerland) than in poor World A countries (like Nepal)?

Conclusion
Some Final Thoughts

Did you know that 85 percent of those living in the 10/40 Window are the poorest of the world's poor?

Yes, missions is broken, and we broke it. It's time now for us to fix it. I have attempted to use my 24 years of experience to illustrate what I have learned from missionaries and national preachers—not to show theories with good intentions, but solutions that work. Some will say that I am anti-missionary, but they won't recall that I am a missionary. If a doctor has a right to complain and warn against "quacks" because they do damage to the people and ruin the name of good doctors; if pastors have a right to preach against compromising, lazy pastors, then why does a missionary not have the right to talk about and warn against those who use his office ineffectively and unbiblically. Why can I be criticized when I go to a church because I "didn't say one word about supporting missionaries"? But on the other hand, it is perfectly acceptable for every missionary since Paul to go to the same churches and ONLY talk about what he is doing or planning to do without ever mentioning the work of the nationals? Why the prejudice, the bigotry, the anger?

It is my hope that you will have learned a little something from all you have had to endure while reading these pages. If you are so inclined, I trust you will contact the Final Frontiers office about supporting a preacher or child or our Smuggler's ministry or enrolling in our missionary training or just going along on a trip. Final Frontiers has nearly a dozen ministry subsidiaries with something of interest for everyone from supporting a preacher, to smuggling Bibles, to buying camels (Saharan bus ministry) for Bedouin Christians to ride to church on.

All that Final Frontiers does is done for three purposes:
- To glorify God
- To benefit His servants
- To bless the giver

I hope we will hear from an army of you readers and that together, through the funding of national preachers, we can boldly preach the Gospel where it has never before been preached.

If you would like to talk to us about supporting a national preacher, we would be delighted to speak with you. On the other hand, if you would like to increase the number of foreign missionaries you or your church already supports, we would be equally delighted to share with you the names and contact information of some worthy American men whom we hope the next generation will emulate in practice, policy, motivation, and methods.

Photo: This Indian hut is made from buffalo dung rather than mud and with a grass thatched roof. In this primitive village located in Andhra Pradesh, the men still hunt with homemade bows and arrows. Since this photo was taken, a majority of the people have converted, and they now have their own church.

[Photo taken January 2008]

APPENDICES

About the Ministry

About the Author

Sources Consulted

Target Groups Where
Foreign Mission Funds Are Spent

- 80 percent for work among those already Christian

- 1.57 percent for work among those already evangelized but still non-Christian.

- 2.5 percent for work among still unevangelized and unreached people groups

If the definition of missions is to preach to the un-reached—those who have never heard the Gospel—and that is how Paul defined missions, then why is only 2.5 percent of the missions funds going for that purpose? Why is 80 percent designated to those who have access to the Gospel or whose societies, like the United States, have been saturated by it?

Appendix A
About Our Ministry

Did you know that there is a difference between the unreached and the un-reachable? In 1989 only four known Christians were living in Mongolia. That country now has an estimated 10,000 indigenous believers.

We at Final Frontiers pledge not to waste your support. For the past three years, according to an outside certified public accounting firm, only 5 percent of our total income was used for administrative purposes, while 95 percent was used for ministry purposes. The foundation is overseen by an executive board of directors made up of fundamental pastors and businessmen. Allow me now to share the various areas of service in which you can partner with Final Frontiers.

National Preacher Sponsorship

Sponsoring a national preacher is a simple process. You can go to our Web site (www.finalfrontiers.org) to choose a preacher or simply tell us which country you are most burdened for, and we will provide you with information on preachers living in that country who are approved for sponsorship and need help. If you do not have a preference, we will assign you a preacher from our most needy list.

Sponsorship is $35 monthly, and since we arrange for most

preachers to have two sponsors, you may have the option of providing a double sponsorship ($70 monthly) if you prefer. The standard $35 sponsorship includes $10 support of the Final Frontiers ministry, which gives our foundation funds with which to operate as well as providing for immediate emergency needs overseas. Typically, up to half of this amount is used overseas.

A sponsor will receive correspondence from his preacher three times annually when Final Frontiers sends your support to your chosen preacher along with his report form.

Each preacher recommended for support has successfully passed through at least three levels of examination and has been proven to be doctrinally sound, morally pure, and have a verifiable track record in church planting and training other men who are serving in the ministry.

TEAM Sponsorship

Sponsorship of a TEAM (**T**ogether **E**ffectively **A**dvancing the **M**inistry) can be done for $10 or more monthly. Though many preachers are being supported, they often collectively lack ministry tools that could be useful. The purpose of the TEAM funding is to provide each country with money to be used for such expenses as printing literature, buying bicycles for the traveling evangelists, building a church or a Bible school, emergency relief, feeding widows, and most often, funding preachers who do not yet have a sponsor.

Each trimester as the funds are mailed abroad, the national coordinator for each nation is asked to fill out a TEAM Report Form which is copied and send to each supporter. This will provide a firsthand report of how funds were effectively used to advance the ministry in that land.

Timothy Sponsorship

Sponsorship of the *Timothy* program is $20 monthly and helps to provide for young men who are serving as an assistant pastor and helping their senior pastor plant churches and train others, while they are still completing their own training. In other words, the Timothy program is in-service training while training for service. These men need support as well, and without it, the poor national pastor has to feed them from his own meager resources.

Touch a Life Sponsorship

Touch a Life provides assistance to an orphaned, abandoned, or destitute child. The $35 monthly sponsorship provides for food, clothing, basic medical care, and educational assistance. All orphanages, home placement programs, and feeding centers assisted by Final Frontiers are administered by pastors who are supported through this foundation and are operated as a ministry of a local church.

Bi-monthly correspondence is required from the children. Funding distribution for the child is identical to that of the preachers (see National Preacher Sponsorship) giving Final Frontiers extra funds to help unsponsored children.

Daily Bread Sponsorship

Daily Bread is a program similar to the Touch a Life Sponsorship but does not have a specific sponsor/child designation; rather, the program involves food bought in bulk to feed unspecified, unsponsored children who are awaiting sponsorship. Donations of any amount are accepted for this great need.

Smugglers Sponsorship

Donations to *Smugglers* are used to purchase and distribute Bibles. Many national pastors and believers do not own a copy of God's Word. Smugglers helps to provide God's Word to those who desire it in free countries and in closed counties such as Islamic nations.

Bags of Hope Sponsorship

Bags of Hope is Final Frontiers' food distribution program, which helps feed widows, orphans, and persecuted families living primarily in the Islamic Middle East. Support for this program is $20 monthly and provides food, clean water, medicine, and vitamins for a family of four.

Home Office Needs

Any offering given for our *Home Office Needs* or for the support of one of our *Missionary Representatives*, whether monthly or a one-time gift, will be applied 100 percent as designated. Other ministry opportunities are announced in Final Frontiers e-mail alerts, on our Facebook page, and in the quarterly *Progress Report*. You may subscribe to this publication free of charge or register to receive it by e-mail.

For more information, contact us at:
Final Frontiers
1200 Peachtree St.
Louisville, GA 30434
800-522-4324
www.finalfrontiers.org

Appendix B
About the Author

Did you know that Christian television programming can now be received in many closed 10/40 Window nations?

J on was born November 18, 1955, the third son to Mack and Nan Nelms, both of whom were first-generation Christians. Though both desired to serve as missionaries, neither felt called to do so. Nan was a school teacher and spent the summers of Jon's youth teaching in "Backyard Bible Clubs." Mack was an employee of Southern Bell and served as a deacon and a trustee in every church in which he was a member, and as a layman he helped to start three churches. Finally at the age of 70, he was ordained as a Baptist pastor and passed away year later. Jon was heavily influenced by both of his parents, who always opened their home to missionaries who were passing through and entertained the family with their stories and experiences.

Jon felt a call to missions at the age of 11 and won his first souls to Christ at the age of 12 and also began preaching at that time. At the age of 15, he began working in the bus ministry and street preaching. At the age of 17 he enrolled in Bible college and graduated 4 years later, the youngest in his class.

Immediately upon graduation, he left for White Plains, New York, with a small group of friends to start the Westchester

County Baptist Church. Two years later he moved to Pomona, California, where he met and married his wife, Juanita Fisher, and became an assistant pastor at the Central Baptist Church. There, for two years, he worked with the youth, served as the bus director, organized the church's camp ministry and street preaching ministry. During that time his son Daniel was born.

Jon's street preaching resulted in the birth of a "park church" of more than 1,000 in weekly attendance that merged with Calvary Baptist Church in Boyle Heights. Jon then moved to Georgia for a short time, seeking God's will and serving as an interim pastor at Hines Baptist Church in Midville, Georgia. The church grew from a handful to nearly 100 in a few months.

Jon declined a permanent position in order to return to California, believing that God would provide a position for him there. After a number of months, he was invited to pastor the Temple City Southern Baptist Church. The name was soon changed to the Believers Baptist Church. It is here that God confirmed his call to missions and used this ministry to break and mold him for that call. It was also there that his daughter Sara was born.

The church sent Jon on several mission trips to Asia in late 1986, where the call was reconfirmed. On the last day of 1986, Jon resigned the church, and four months later, after they had called a new pastor, he moved to Georgia after having legally incorporated the Final Frontiers Foundation. At that time the ministry was supporting preachers in Thailand only. Since then the foundation has sponsored more than 1,400 preachers in 84 nations. These men collectively have started (as of February 2011) more than 36,000 churches, averaging a new church being started every 3 hours and 26 minutes.

In 2006 Juanita passed on to Heaven after 28 years of marriage, leaving her imprint on Jon, their children, and the ministry. A month later Sara was married to Michael Horne, a British ministry employee, and they have a daughter Jennifer. A few months later Daniel was married to Nolvia Aguirre from

Honduras, and they have two daughters, Valentina and Elizabeth. In May 2008 Jon was married to Nolin Vargas, a Honduran ministry employee who now travels with him worldwide and is a great asset to his ministry and life.

Jon is a 1977 graduate of Hyles-Anderson College and has received an honorary D.D. from his alma mater and a Doctorate in Missiology from the Fundamental Baptist College for Asia

Bible Translation Availability

- At least some part of Scripture has been translated into 2,212 of the world's 6,500 languages

- 366 languages have the entire Bible

- 928 other languages have the New Testament

- Individual books (e.g., the Gospel of John) are available in 918 additional languages

- 80 percent of the world's people have access to at least some portion of the Bible in a language they can understand.

Non-Christian countries have more than 227 million Bibles within their borders—more than needed to serve all the Christians living in them, but they do not because they have been poorly distributed.

Thousands of language groups do not have a SINGLE page of the Bible in their language.

98.7% of people have access to Scripture in 6,700 languages, leaving 78 million in 6,800 languages with no access at all.

Scripture Distribution Per Year

Total Distribution . . . . 4,600 million pieces

World A . . . . 20 million (0.4%)

World B . . . . 680 million (14.5%)

World C . . . . 3,900 million (84.8%)

Appendix C
Sources Consulted

Good news! Missions researcher David Barrett says the country with the most rapid Christian expansion ever is China, where there are 10,000 new Christian converts every day!

Books

Allen, Roland. *Missionary Methods—St. Paul's or Ours?*. Cambridge: The Lutterworth Press, 2006.

Barrett, David and Todd Johnson. World Christian Trends. Pasadena: William Carey Library Publishers, 2003.

Johnstone, Patrick. *Operation World*. Grand Rapids: Zondervan Publishing Company, 1993.

Legg, John. *John G. Paton/Five Pioneer Missionaries*. Edinburgh: The Banner of Truth Trust, 1965.

Richardson, Don. *Eternity in Their Hearts*. Ventura: Regal Books, G.L. Publications, 1981.

Yohannon, K.P. *Revolution in World Missions*. Altamonte Springs: Creation House Publishers, 1986.

Internet
Dom.imb.org/The%20Unfinished%20Task.htm
Emptytomb.org/research
Gem-werc.com/gd/listings
Generousgiving.org
globalchristianity.org
Gmi.org/research/database.htm
Gordonconwell.edu/ockengaglobalchristianity/
resources.php
Home.snu.edu
Imb.org/globalresearch
Jesus.org.uk
Joshuaproject.net
Justinlong.org
Lausanneworldpulse.com
Missions Mobilizer
Momentum-mag.org/wiki/Main_Page
Operationworld.org
Peoplegroups.org
Peopleteams.org
Scribd.com
Wholesomewords.org/missions